Earth **Science**

Discovering the secrets of the earth

MINERALS

Atlantic Europe Publishing

Wulfenite

Ruby

 **Atlantic Europe Publishing**

First published in 2000 by
Atlantic Europe Publishing Company Ltd
Copyright © 2000
Atlantic Europe Publishing Company Ltd

Author
Brian Knapp, BSc, PhD

Art Director
Duncan McCrae, BSc

Editors
Mary Sanders, BSc and Gillian Gatehouse

Illustrations
David Woodroffe and Julian Baker

Designed and produced by
EARTHSCAPE EDITIONS

Reproduced in Malaysia by
Global Colour

Printed in Hong Kong by
Wing King Tong Company Ltd

Suggested cataloguing location
Knapp, Brian
    Earth Sciences set of 8 volumes
    Volume 1: *Minerals*
    1. Geology – Juvenile Literature
    2. Geography – Juvenile Literature
    550
ISBN 1 862140 33 2

Picture credits
All photographs are from the Earthscape Editions
photolibrary.

*This product is manufactured from sustainable managed
forests. For every tree cut down, at least one more is
planted.*

Citrine

Contents

Chapter 1: Mineral forming environments

Except in isolated places where volcanoes pour out fiery liquids, the earth's surface is solid. Only a tiny fraction of the solid surface is made from living matter (for example, coal). The vast majority of the earth's surface is made from solid, non-living (inorganic) material. We call it ROCK.

Look more closely at a rock, and you will find that it is, in turn, made from a small number of materials with a definite and precise chemical formula. They are MINERALS. Minerals are, therefore, the basic building blocks of the earth.

(Left) In cavities filled with fluids crystals begin to form. Many substances crystallise out from these hidden 'Aladdin's caves' inside the ground, and all compete for the same space. Here you can see quartz, the glassy mineral, another form of quartz called citrine and an iron oxide called haematite.

(Above) Amethyst crystals have grown on the inside of the cavity.

These crystals grew by adding sheets of molecules to the leading faces of the needle-shaped crystals. Many crystals grow in this way, becoming ever longer, as you can see on page 6.

(Right) Crystals can grow in a liquid provided the solution is saturated with suitable materials.

(Below) A GEODE is a nodule that represents a cavity in a rock in which minerals were able to form. Splitting open the geode reveals the crystals growing inward. The geode is not filled because the source of minerals was used up before that could happen.

Under the right conditions (see picture right) all minerals can form CRYSTALS, which are regular geometrical shapes, such as cubes and prisms. Most minerals are very small and can only be seen with a microscope. Only occasionally do they grow to a size at which they can be seen with the naked eye.

When minerals grow large, and especially when they make geometrical shapes, they can look very beautiful. Some minerals (including those that do not form crystals) are thought to be particularly attractive, and they are called GEMS. Diamonds and salt are examples of minerals. A diamond is made only of the ELEMENT carbon. A diamond is also an example of a gem. Salt is the compound sodium chloride, made up of sodium and chloride IONS. Salt crystals are not regarded as gems.

More than 3000 minerals are known, but many of them are rare. This book focuses on the more common minerals and, in particular, on those that are the main rock-forming minerals or those that are important for use in industry.

(*Right*) Smoky quartz crystals have grown on the inside of the cavity. Notice the base plate from which they are forming.

Mineralogists call these needle-shaped crystals PRISMATIC.

Minerals and the earth's structure

To understand the origin of the minerals which we now find in the rocks, we need to look back into the early history of the earth, when the entire planet was molten. At this time there was an opportunity for elements to separate, with some of the denser elements sinking and the lighter ones rising to the surface. As a result, the CORE of the earth consists mainly of the metal elements iron and nickel.

Similarly, some elements become concentrated in the MANTLE, the shell of rocks that now surrounds the core. This region became dominated by the elements silicon and magnesium.

The upper mantle is mostly mobile and, in some places, actually liquid. It is the source of most oceanic volcanic rocks. The upper mantle consists mostly of minerals that contain iron and magnesium as well as silicon. Any rocks that contain high proportions of iron and magnesium are dark in colour. Dark-coloured minerals of this kind are called FERROMAGNESIAN MINERALS, of which OLIVINE, AUGITE, and HORNBLENDE are examples. (For more details on these minerals see pages 53, 56, and 57.)

When mantle material rises to the surface, it is known as MAGMA. Magma that rises in the oceans mainly solidifies into the rock BASALT. Basalt contains ferromagnesian minerals together with another mineral called FELDSPAR.

During the early stages of the formation of the earth a kind of solid 'scum' began to form. It was made of lighter minerals that floated on the surface of the mantle. In this way the CRUST began to form. It was made mainly of the lightest elements, silicon and aluminium. Rocks that are mostly silicon and aluminium tend to be light in colour. Most volcanoes that come to the surface through the continental crust are not made of mantle material, but of recycled crust (for more information on this see the book *Earthquakes and Volcanoes* in the *Earth Science set*) and they, too, contain light-coloured minerals.

Whether they are dark, and begin in the mantle, or light, and come from the crust, the vast majority of the minerals we find on the surface contain silicon. They are known as SILICATES. Most minerals that we find belong to the crust and contain both aluminium and silicon.

As you can see, the continental crust is a complicated mixture of molten material from the mantle and remelted material from the crust. It, therefore, contains a wider range of minerals than

(Below) This diagram shows the three main structural zones of the earth: the core, which is mostly nickel and iron and is sometimes called the NiFe zone, after the chemical symbols for the elements; the mantle, which is mainly silicon and magnesium and sometimes called the SiMa; and the thin crust, where the minerals are mainly silicon and aluminium, and which is, therefore, sometimes referred to as the SiAl zone.

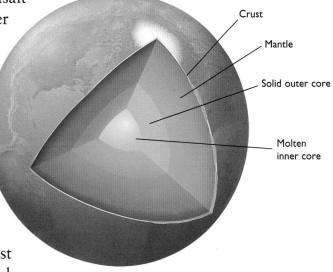

Crust

Mantle

Solid outer core

Molten inner core

(Below) Dark augite crystals in basalt.

the ocean floor. In fact, because it is a mixture of rocks from different environments, the continental crust contains by far the most varied range of minerals on earth.

Mineral-forming environments

A mineral-forming environment is a place where minerals are made. Some minerals form at the surface – for example, the clay minerals that make up the world's shale rocks – others form at shallow depths within rocks, and some form deep within the crust. Some form as a result of precipitation from solutions, some grow from molten rock, and some are formed deep below the surface where the rocks are very hot and under high pressure.

The crust contains a huge variety of minerals because there are many different kinds of environment in which minerals can form. The main environments, however, can be classified as volcanic (igneous), heat and pressure (metamorphic), and surface deposit (sedimentary). These are described below.

(Below) Light-coloured minerals dominate this continental granite. The white opaque mineral is ORTHOCLASE FELDSPAR. The pink opaque mineral is PLAGIOCLASE FELDSPAR. The black needle-shaped crystals are hornblende, and the small shiny plate-like minerals are BIOTITE MICA. The glassy greyish material filling in the spaces is QUARTZ.

The diagram labels:

New mountain system

Low-pressure metamorphic rocks

Igneous rocks

Sedimentary rocks

Old metamorphic and igneous rocks of stable continent

High-temperature and -pressure metamorphic rocks

Erosion

Plate moves down

(Below) This diagram shows the main mineral-forming environments.

Volcanic (igneous) environments

The materials from which all the earth's surface minerals and rocks were originally made is the liquid called magma. Some magma reaches the surface as volcanic eruptions. Most, however, never gets to the surface, but solidifies underground. Volcanic (surface) rocks are known as EXTRUSIVE ROCKS, while those that remain buried are called INTRUSIVE ROCKS. Together, they make up the great class of rocks called IGNEOUS ROCKS. They contain a wealth of different minerals and are among the most mineral-rich environments on earth.

The nature of magma

Magma is not an even mixture, but appears to be very variable in the proportion of elements it contains. As a result, the range of minerals formed from cooled magma also varies widely.

Magma normally moves into the continental crust during a period of mountain building. For example, if two continental PLATES collide, and one plate is partly forced under the other, or if part of the thin ocean floor collides with a thick continental plate and is entirely overridden, the downward-moving material

(Above) Lava cools quickly without giving minerals much chance to grow. Thus, while basalt is still made of crystals, they are too small to see with the naked eye.

melts. This molten material, which may contain rocks from both the continent and the ocean floor, slowly melts and then rises like a plume into the continental crust above.

Magma does not rise simply by pushing rock aside, but rather by melting the rock above and around it. This is why the magma contains such a wide variety of minerals, and why it is so variable from one place to another.

(Below) This diagram shows some of the mineral forming environments associated with igneous activity.

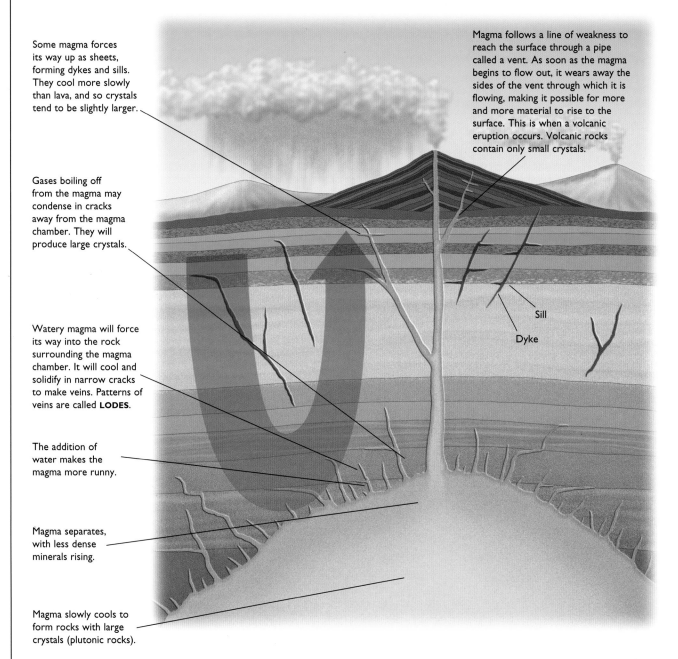

Some magma forces its way up as sheets, forming dykes and sills. They cool more slowly than lava, and so crystals tend to be slightly larger.

Magma follows a line of weakness to reach the surface through a pipe called a vent. As soon as the magma begins to flow out, it wears away the sides of the vent through which it is flowing, making it possible for more and more material to rise to the surface. This is when a volcanic eruption occurs. Volcanic rocks contain only small crystals.

Gases boiling off from the magma may condense in cracks away from the magma chamber. They will produce large crystals.

Sill

Dyke

Watery magma will force its way into the rock surrounding the magma chamber. It will cool and solidify in narrow cracks to make veins. Patterns of veins are called **LODES**.

The addition of water makes the magma more runny.

Magma separates, with less dense minerals rising.

Magma slowly cools to form rocks with large crystals (plutonic rocks).

Above the magma chamber

The variety in the magma is only one reason why igneous rocks are so variable in the minerals they contain. The other reason lies in the region that the magma reaches as it gets close to the surface.

The magma chamber exerts an enormous pressure on the surrounding rocks, causing those near the upper surface of the chamber to buckle upwards. This creates weaknesses between the rock layers and also makes the rocks crack. The cracks vary enormously in size and can be simply hairline or fissures many tens of centimetres across; but they are extremely important because they are routes that the magma can follow.

Large cracks allow molten magma to rush to the surface as a volcanic eruption. This material cools quickly in the air and, therefore, rarely contains any sizeable crystals. Much of the material remains in a glassy form. Some LAVA and most ASH tends to be glassy.

Lava and ash are the only extrusive rocks. Most magma cools underground as an intrusive rock or as some other kind of deposit. Substantial amounts of magma can be forced between layers of overlying

(Below) This diagram shows where minerals can be found in a landscape after the mountains have been partly removed by erosion.

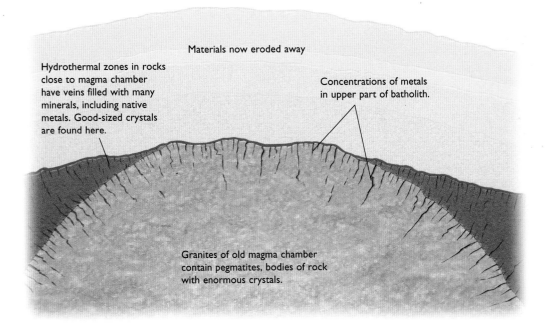

Materials now eroded away

Hydrothermal zones in rocks close to magma chamber have veins filled with many minerals, including native metals. Good-sized crystals are found here.

Concentrations of metals in upper part of batholith.

Granites of old magma chamber contain pegmatites, bodies of rock with enormous crystals.

rocks (making SILLS) or cut across them (making DYKES). The magma cools less quickly in these situations than in the air; but if the sills or dykes are thin, they will still cool relatively quickly because they are in direct contact with cooler rock. Crystals in sills and dykes tend, as a result, to be quite small.

Many changes take place to minerals within the body of the magma, both while it is still melting its way upwards and later, when it cools. During the early period the less dense minerals tend to rise to the top, and the heavier minerals tend to sink. As a result, the magma divides.

Water is also an important part of many magmas. One of the important things about the presence of water is to make magma very much more runny (less VISCOUS). The least dense parts of the mixture, containing the highest water content, are near the top of the magma chamber. They become very runny materials. The most runny materials of all are called VOLATILES. Because they are so runny, they are able to force their way into small cracks in the overlying rocks, a vital process in the formation of many minerals.

When volatiles reach cooler conditions away from the magma chamber, the liquids or gases solidify, and

(Below) Pumice, a frothy form of lava, contains no crystals. It is a glassy substance.

(Below) This basalt rock was part of a sill. It cooled before crystals could grow, and its small crystals can be seen only with a microscope.

crystals begin to form. The infilling of minerals that form from this watery part of the magma is called a **HYDROTHERMAL DEPOSIT** (hydrothermal meaning 'hot water'). It is often the most rich of the crystal forming environments.

The order in which crystals form is determined by the temperature and the chemistry of the volatile. As each new crystal forms, it takes some atoms from the mixture, leaving what remains with a changed composition. It is from this changed composition that the next crystals begin to form. This process continues until all the minerals have formed, and the magma has solidified.

In some places the volatiles boil off, and superhot gases move into the rocks above the mantle. These gases tend to condense as crystals on the walls of any cavities they reach, growing outward much as stalactites grow down from the roof of a cave. These environments often produce the biggest and most finely shaped mineral crystals. Such locations are often called **PEGMATITE VEINS**.

(Above) If mineral-forming atoms in the liquid are used up before the cavity can be filled with growing crystals, a space with sharp-pointed crystals results. Minerals that have grown into such cavities can be geometrically perfect.

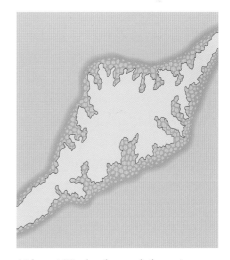

(Above) Hydrothermal deposits form in spaces within the rock. They grow as crystals surrounded by liquid.

Within the magma chamber

The magma remaining in the magma chamber may take tens of millions of years to cool, and so there are better opportunities for larger crystals to grow. These deep-seated PLUTONIC ROCKS, such as granite, often contain large crystals.

Minerals from igneous environments

The minerals expected to be found in volcanic rocks like basalt are plagioclase feldspar, augite and hornblende. The common minerals in granites consist primarily of feldspar and quartz.

Hydrothermal deposits contain large amounts of sulphide minerals, such as chalcopyrite, galena, molybdenite, pyrite, and sphalerite. Calcite and fluorite are also common.

(Below and left) The common rock-forming minerals in igneous rocks are: feldspars, micas, hornblende, augite, olivine, and quartz.

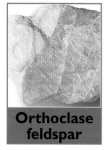
Orthoclase feldspar

Biotite mica

Hornblende

Augite

Olivine

Quartz

Mountain building environments

Mountains are formed largely from sediments that have been laid down under the oceans and compressed into rocks. They are called sedimentary rocks. When the earth's tectonic plates collide, the immense pressure placed on these sediments makes them buckle up. Not only is there direct pressure from colliding tectonic plates, but the buckling also forces some of the sediments deeper into the earth, where it is extremely hot.

Furthermore, magma often flows deep into the heart of these folded rocks, adding even more heat.

The METAMORPHIC ROCKS of mountains are, therefore, often the results both of great pressure and high temperature. Yet despite this, the majority of the mountain rocks do not melt. Instead, although they

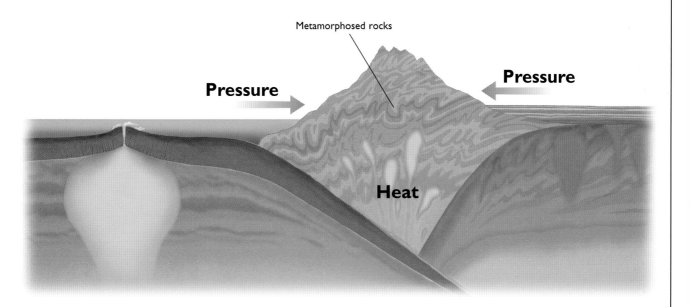

Metamorphosed rocks

Pressure →

← **Pressure**

Heat

remain solid, under such intense conditions atoms in them move as though they were in a liquid (as they do, for example, in white hot steel).

A wide range of minerals (such as kyanite) forms in these conditions, many of which cannot even form directly when the rock is molten.

The effect of temperature and pressure on rocks during mountain building is enormous. Many kinds of metamorphism occur, and each gives a different range of minerals. Broadly, they can be grouped as contact metamorphism and regional metamorphism.

Contact metamorphism
Minerals that form from contact with magma chambers are the result of temperature rather than pressure. The heat involved is quite localised and does not normally make the rocks produce large crystals.

Regional metamorphism
In some places the main changes come about simply as a result of the effect of pressure. This normally happens in rocks close to the surface or on the edges of the main mountain-building zone. One of the most important minerals that forms in these low-temperature, medium-pressure conditions is

(Above) This diagram shows the variety of metamorphic environments in which minerals can be created. The highest degree of metamorphism occurs deep within the mountains, where heat and pressure are greatest. Here, large mineral grains occur within gneiss rocks. Lower degrees of metamorphism produce schist rocks in which most minerals are small plates, but large minerals, such as garnets, also form.

(Above) This is a baked clay rock, called a hornfels. The crystals in it are too small to be seen with the naked eye. As heating becomes more intense, the first stages of change are found when the rocks become 'spotted'.

MUSCOVITE MICA. It grows as small, platy crystals that spread at right angles to the direction of pressure. With little pressure, small crystals grow in shale rocks that were formerly made of clay minerals. Low-pressure rocks containing micas of this kind are SLATES.

When the pressure and temperature are higher, the micas have more opportunity to grow to be larger, although they rarely become as large as they do in igneous rocks. The rocks produced at this stage are called SCHISTS.

Temperature and pressure are also so severe that new minerals begin to grow among the micas. Conspicuous in many schists are red garnets and blue kyanite crystals.

(Below and left) The common rock-forming minerals in metamorphic rocks are: quartz, feldspars, hornblende, augite, micas, GARNET, and CHLORITE.

Quartz

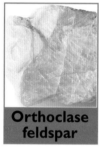

Orthoclase feldspar

Hornblende

Augite

Biotite mica

Garnet

(Below) The sheen is characteristic of thousands of mica crystals lying in the same plane.

Chlorite

In regions of even higher temperature and pressure the minerals of the former rock break down completely and reorganise into bands of new minerals. The dominant mineral in this case is quartz. The rocks are made of bands of minerals and are called GNEISS.

Many of the minerals in metamorphic zones are, however, the result of hydrothermal activity as liquids from magma chambers cool. They are described on pages 12 and 13.

Sedimentary environments

All mountains are gradually attacked by the forces of the weather and reduced to small fragments. The fragments are, in turn, carried by rivers to the oceans, where they settle out in calm waters to form layers of sediment. The rocks that form are sedimentary rocks.

New minerals form during weathering, but few are spectacularly large like those created in igneous or metamorphic environments. Quite the contrary, minerals that form during weathering are usually microscopically small. Thus, for example, feldspar, the most common mineral in igneous rocks, weathers to clay minerals no more than a few millionths of a metre across.

(Above) This is a piece of petrified wood. It is a crystalline replacement deposit. What was once organic material is now silica. This material has no crystals in it. It is CRYSTALLINE.

(Below) The environments in which minerals form within sedimentary rocks. Some crystals grow in surface deposits, such as salt, but most form in sediments from percolating mineral-carrying waters. Some form in rock nodules called geodes.

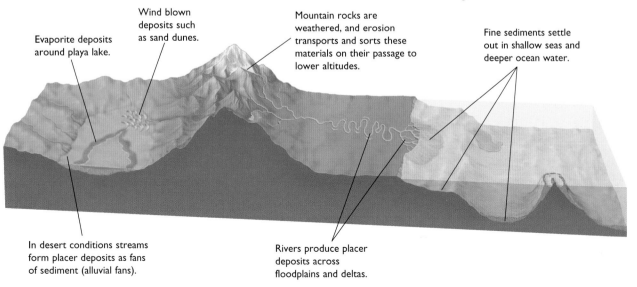

Evaporite deposits around playa lake.

Wind blown deposits such as sand dunes.

Mountain rocks are weathered, and erosion transports and sorts these materials on their passage to lower altitudes.

Fine sediments settle out in shallow seas and deeper ocean water.

In desert conditions streams form placer deposits as fans of sediment (alluvial fans).

Rivers produce placer deposits across floodplains and deltas.

New mineral GRAINS (irregularly shaped pieces of mineral rather than crystals) do form in this environment as waters seep through the sediments, DISSOLVING some minerals and PRECIPITATING the material elsewhere. Iron oxide, iron sulphide, lead sulphide and quartz all move in this way. If such materials occupy the spaces formerly held by fossils or natural cavities, they can then form crystals of large size.

In the shallow seas by the coast and in inland lakes, the dissolved minerals in water can crystallise. These are concentrated by evaporation and so are called EVAPORITE MINERALS. They include salt and gypsum. Limestones are the remains of the skeletons of living things. New minerals form here, too, as the sediment compacts into limestone. Calcite and dolomite are especially common.

(Below) Halite crystals from an evaporite deposit.

Quartz

Calcite

Dolomite

Clay minerals

Halite

Gypsum

Placer deposits

Placer deposits are a form of sediment. They occur when weathered material is being carried by rivers. The natural weathering of the rocks often releases minerals separately, so that a rock containing, for example, gold, will break down releasing the grains of gold as NATIVE METAL. Because gold is so much more dense than most minerals, the river naturally separates the gold particles, carrying the lighter weight minerals to the sea, and allowing the heavier minerals to remain on the river bed. Thus, rivers provide a natural way of sieving one kind of mineral from another. River alluvium, or coastal sediments with high concentrations of heavy metals, are called PLACER DEPOSITS.

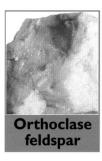
Orthoclase feldspar

(Above and right) The common rock-forming minerals in sedimentary rocks are: quartz, CALCITE, DOLOMITE, clay minerals, HALITE, GYPSUM, and feldspars.

(Below) This gleaming white mineral deposit is travertine. It has been formed when minerals precipitate from waters as they cool. Mammoth Hot Springs, Yellowstone National Park, Wyoming, USA.

Chapter 2: Identifying minerals

Because there are so many minerals, it can be challenging to identify one you might have collected. It may even be difficult to decide whether the sample is actually a mineral or a rock. To help with this, geologists use a number of properties of minerals. This chapter describes the main physical properties that are useful to people without special equipment. For example, minerals have characteristic colours, some are harder than others, and so on. Nevertheless, because minerals are naturally quite variable, in this particular area of earth science, experience is important. By looking at a number of specimens, it is easier to see the range of variation involved.

Here are some of the simple properties that can be used to identify a mineral.

Colour

Colour is often one of the most striking features of a mineral. For example, sulphur is often a bright primrose yellow, and azurite is often deep blue. The difficulty with colour is that it is not a very reliable indicator of a mineral because the colour is affected by the tiny amounts of IMPURITIES (that

(Below) Iron pyrite is a golden yellow colour.

(Below) Citrine is yellow-brown.

(Below) Fluorite is purple.

(Below) Smoky quartz is brown or grey.

(Below) Malachite is a distinctive green.

(Above) Sulphur is commonly yellow.

(Right) Azurite is a blue colour.

is, the variety of metal ions, such as iron and magnesium) in the mineral. Diamonds and quartz are just two minerals that have a wide range of colours. Pure quartz is colourless. It is called rock crystal. But if it contains the impurity iron, it will be violet (and called amethyst). If it has been close to a source of radioactivity it also changes its colour to make a brown smoky quartz. So, although the colour changes are dramatic, the mineral is still quartz.

Streak

STREAK is the colour of the ground-up powder from a mineral. The powder is commonly produced by rubbing the mineral on a white unglazed porcelain plate (the back of a wall tile, for example). Because this rubbing action produces a coloured line, or streak, on the plate, the property is called the streak.

Streak is very useful for identifying dark-coloured minerals. For example, zinc sulphide and lead sulphide often look similar, but zinc sulphide streaks brown, while lead sulphide streaks grey-black. However, minerals with a hardness greater than the streak plate (about 6.5) cannot be tested this way, and it is difficult to distinguish between the many minerals that streak white.

(Below) The 'lead' of a pencil is no more than the streak of a mineral put to good use. It is graphite. It streaks grey-black.

(Below) Orpiment looks yellow and streaks lemon yellow.

(Below) Haematite looks brick red and streaks brown.

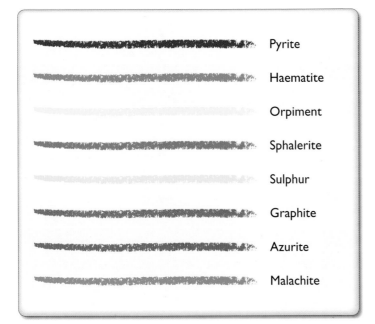

Pyrite

Haematite

Orpiment

Sphalerite

Sulphur

Graphite

Azurite

Malachite

(Below) Chalcopyrite looks yellow and streaks black.

Lustre

Lustre is the way in which a mineral surface reflects light. The categories normally used include metallic, resinous, vitreous (looks like broken glass), and adamantine (sparkles like a gem). You can usually tell the lustre of a mineral only by looking at the way light plays off crystal surfaces.

(Above) Lead has a metallic lustre.

Hardness

Hardness gives a guide as to how well a mineral resists scratching. The scale for determining hardness is called Mohs' scale, after the German mineralogist Frederick Mohs, who developed the scale in the early 19th century.

The reference scale is made up of commonly available minerals of appropriate hardness. Notice that it is not an even scale, simply a way of putting minerals into hardness categories. Thus, diamond is not ten times harder than talc; it is immeasurably harder. The softest mineral used for the scale is talc and it is allocated a hardness of **1**. Gypsum is the test substance for hardness **2**, calcite for hardness **3**, fluorite for hardness **4**, apatite for hardness **5**, feldspar for hardness **6**, quartz for hardness **7**, topaz for hardness **8**, corundum for hardness **9**, and diamond for hardness **10**. Diamond is the hardest mineral in the world. So, for example, if a mineral is scratched by topaz (**8**) but scratches quartz (**7**), its hardness is between **7** and **8**, usually written as **7½**. Minerals are assigned a hardness of either a whole number or half a number.

A standard Mohs' testing kit is normally used by geologists, although other more readily available substances can also be used. For example, a penknife blade is about hardness **6** and a thumbnail about **2½**. A copper coin is about **3½**.

(Above) Rose quartz has a vitreous lustre.

Mohs' Scale of Hardness

1 Talc
2 Gypsum
3 Calcite
4 Fluorite
5 Apatite
6 Orthoclase feldspar
7 Quartz
8 Topaz
9 Corundum
10 Diamond

Calcite = **3**

Quartz = **7**

Fluorite = **4**

Topaz = **8**

Talc = **1**

Corundum = **9**

Apatite = **5**

Gypsum = **2**

Fingernail = **2½**

Orthoclase feldspar = **6**

Diamond = **10**

23

Specific gravity

Specific gravity is the weight of a sample relative to the weight of an equal volume of water. Metallic minerals generally have high values for specific gravity (5 or more) compared to non-metallic minerals (about 2–3).

Certain minerals are readily distinguished by their specific gravity, of which barium compounds are perhaps the most important, being very heavy.

Transparency

Minerals vary in the amount of light they will transmit. If light will pass right through a mineral, it is called TRANSPARENT. If light passes through it, but no clear image can be seen on the other side, then it is TRANSLUCENT. If it does not allow light to pass through it, but reflects all light reaching the surface, then it is OPAQUE.

(Below) In this sample of apophylite clusters set on quartz the bladed crystals have a pearly lustre and are translucent, while the quartz is colourless and transparent. The small white crystals are opaque.

Quartz

Apophylite

(Below) This is a combination of sphalerite, zinc ore, which looks black and streaks brown, and pyrite, which looks brassy yellow and streaks greenish-black. Both minerals are opaque, that is, they reflect the light. Small crystals of colourless transparent quartz can also be seen.

Cleavage

Cleavage is the way a mineral breaks along certain lines of weakness. The pattern of cleavage is related to the structure of the crystal faces, which, in turn, is related to the way atoms are arranged in the mineral. Minerals that break cleanly and evenly have a perfect cleavage. Those that break less well have good, distinct, and poor cleavages. Some minerals have no cleavage at all.

Fracture

Fracture is the way a mineral breaks when it does not cleave. It is especially relevant to minerals that are glassy in character. They normally fracture with an uneven or conchoidal (that is, shell-like) curved fracture.

(Above) Muscovite showing perfect cleavage that creates the flakes so typical of this mineral.

(Left) Uneven fracture in aquamarine. The surface has a vitreous lustre.

Crystal form

Crystal form is the geometrical shape that the mineral normally occupies. It gives minerals much of their attraction, but it is also one of the best ways of identifying them.

The crystal form, like the cleavage, is determined by the atomic structure of the mineral.

Minerals are classified into six crystal systems, each a mathematical geometric form.

As in mathematics, the crystal form is described by imaginary AXES OF SYMMETRY. In this classification the system with the greatest symmetry (the cubic system) is first. The other systems are organised so that the one with the least symmetry is last.

Many of these shapes are described as prisms. In this context, a prism is an elongated shape, rather like toothpaste squeezed from a tube.

Cubic (also called isometric). Crystals grow as cubes, and all three axes are of equal length and at right angles.

Tetragonal. Crystals have three axes at right angles, two the same length. Many tetragonal crystals have four-sided pyramids at their ends.

Hexagonal. Crystals have three axes of symmetry, all in the same plane, and a fourth axis at right angles to the other three. Crystals have a six-sided base and are often needle-like. The ends are often rounded. (Sometimes a 'trigonal' system is also recognised, but it is very similar to hexagonal).

Orthorhombic. A rhomboid is a three dimensional parallelogram. Crystals have three unequal axes, all at right angles to each other. They often occur as rhombohedrons and pyramids, as well as prisms.

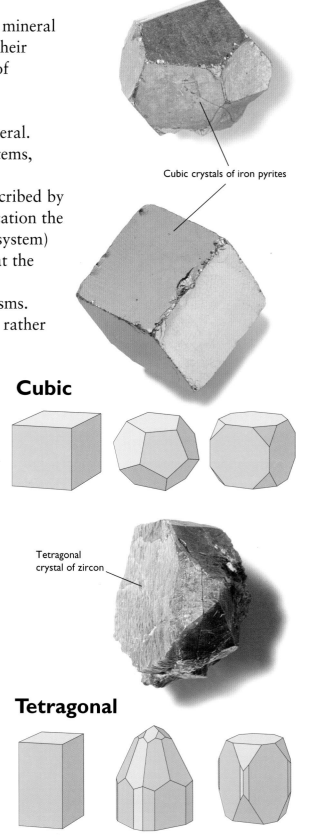

Cubic crystals of iron pyrites

Cubic

Tetragonal crystal of zircon

Tetragonal

Monoclinic. Three unequal axes, two at right angles, with the third at an angle to the other two. These crystals are usually prisms.

Triclinic. Three unequal axes, no axis at right angles to any other. These crystals are often flattened with thin cross-sections.

Monoclinic

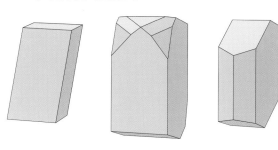

Monoclinic crystals of gypsum

Hexagonal

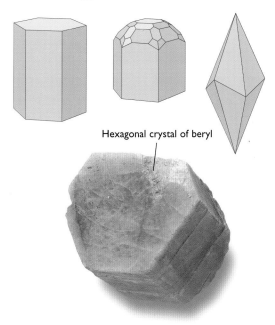

Hexagonal crystal of beryl

Triclinic

Triclinic crystals of kyanite

Orthorhombic

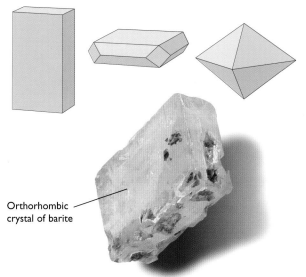

Orthorhombic crystal of barite

(Below) Aragonite, showing twinning.

Twinned crystals

Crystals grow more commonly as composites, or groups of crystals, than they do singly. When one crystal grows against or through another, it is called a twin crystal. Often these patterns of twinning are characteristic of a particular mineral.

There are three types of twin crystals: contact twins, penetration twins, and repeated twins. In a contact twin, the twinned crystals share a face; in penetration twins the crystals grow through one another; in repeated twinning, crystals grow back to back in a regular way.

(Below) Selenite (moonstone; gypsum) showing penetration twins.

Habit

Each mineral often takes on a typical shape, or form. This preferred way that crystals grow is called the habit. Typical habits include bladed (blade-shaped), prismatic (drawn out into a needle), and tabular (plate-like).

Tabular wulfenite

Striated pyrite

Prismatic ruby

Dendritic copper

Reniform haematite

Bladed stibnite

Equant halite

Chapter 3: Classifying minerals

The names of minerals have many origins. A few are so old that their meaning is now obscure. Many more were named as they were discovered, either using Greek or Latin words. Often the Greek or Latin word describes some special characteristic of the minerals. Sometimes, minerals are named for the place where they were first found, or even named after a scientist.

Minerals are divided up, or classified, into groups based on their chemical composition. In many ways it is similar to the classification used for living things, each mineral with a definite crystal structure being given a species name, with additional names added for specially distinctive characteristics. This is particularly useful because minerals with similar chemistry tend to be formed in similar environments. You will notice this as you look at the examples in the book.

To understand how the classification works, it is helpful to know that minerals are normally made of charged particles, called ions. Most minerals contain a metal ion bonded to a non-metal ion. The metal ion may be, for example, calcium, and the non-metal ion may be carbonate. Thus, the mineral calcite is chemically calcium carbonate. It is the non-metal ion that gives most of the characteristics to the mineral, with the metal ion simply adding more subtle variation to the properties (such as colour). As a result, the classification of minerals is based on the non-metal ion (anion), and minerals are classified as oxides, carbonates, and so on.

THE HISTORY OF INVESTIGATING MINERALS

The science of studying minerals (mineralogy) has a long history because people have always been attracted to the colour and shape of crystals. One of the earliest people to make a study of minerals was Georg Bauer, more widely known as Agricola. He wrote books on metals as early as 1556. Nicolaus Steno discovered that the angles between faces in a crystal are always the same for a given mineral. In 1784, Rene Just Hauy, suggested that all minerals, no matter what their size, build up from identical tiny crystals. This is why the faces of crystals always have the same angles.

Abraham Gottlob Werner then found a method of identifying crystals by physical characteristics (what they look like, how hard they are, and the like).

Because all minerals have a definite chemical formula, the study of minerals has gone hand in hand with the study of chemistry. In 1837 James Dana produced the first classification of minerals based on their chemical composition. It is still the most widely used and the one used in this book.

The science of chemistry developed rapidly in the early 19th century, as did the figuring out of minerals, especially through the efforts of Jons Berzelius.

As new techniques and types of microscope were developed, it became possible to cut rocks into slices so thin that they became transparent. By using a special (polarizing) microscope on these thin sections of rock, it became possible to identify minerals by looking for the way minerals bend (refract) light. Today X-rays are used in a more precise way to look at the structure of minerals.

Native elements

The simplest class of minerals is the native elements. Each one of them is an element in the Periodic Table that can be found in nature in its native, or pure, state.

Native elements are found uncombined because they are not very reactive.

Native elements can be grouped as: metals, semi-metals, and non-metals.

The native metals include gold, silver, copper, platinum, and iron. Semi-metals include arsenic and bismuth. Non-metals include sulphur and carbon (in the forms of diamond and graphite).

Copper

Copper Cu
Colour: Copper-red, tarnishing to brown, green, and black
Hardness: 3
Cleavage: None
Crystals: Cubic
Other: Specific gravity 9, a moderately heavy metal

Copper was one of the first metals to be used in the ancient world. Its name comes from the Latin, *cuprum*, which means 'metal of Cyprus', an island in the Mediterranean Sea where the Romans had large copper mines.

Native copper is often found in basalt rocks and in veins that were once close to magma chambers. The shape of a piece of native copper reflects the deep underground fissures in which it was originally deposited. The picture on the right shows a piece with a branching pattern.

The largest piece of native copper ever found was in Minesota Mine, Michigan, USA. It weighed over 500 tonnes.

This native copper sample is mingled with the surrounding rock.

Diamond

Carbon C

Colour: White, colourless, and pale shades of other colours

Streak: None (it is harder than all other substances)

Hardness: 10

Cleavage: Perfect

Crystals: Cubic

Other: Specific gravity 3.5

Diamond, named from the Greek word *adamas*, meaning invincible, is far more rare than graphite. Diamonds were formed under immense temperatures and pressures, such as found in pipes leading to ancient volcanoes. The most famous diamond mine, at Kimberley, South Africa, follows an old volcanic pipe for more than two kilometres vertically into the earth. Diamonds are also found as placer deposits.

Carbon atoms can link to form a very stable mineral. Diamonds have atoms so tightly bonded together that they are one of the hardest substances known.

Pure diamond is colourless and transparent. It commonly forms a shape like two pyramids base to base (a tetrahedron). Jewellers make use of this property when they cleave rough diamonds to make jewellery. Each of the faces (called FACETS) is created by splitting the diamond parallel to the faces of its crystals.

Diamond is not always colourless; if it contains impurities, it may be a darker colour. Some diamonds are almost black.

This piece of Kimberlite rock shows the way that most diamond occurs, as a dull yellowish mineral set in a rock background. This diamond is translucent and highly flawed. Only occasionally does a transparent and flawless piece of mineral occur. The cut diamond placed on the rock shows the comparison.

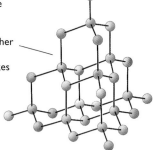

This diagram represents the structure of diamond. It is built of interlocking carbon atoms with no room for other atoms to form part of the structure. That is what makes the mineral so unreactive.

Gold

Gold Au

Colour: Gold-yellow

Streak: Gold-yellow

Hardness: 3

Cleavage: None

Crystals: Cubic

Other: Specific gravity 15–19 (very heavy)

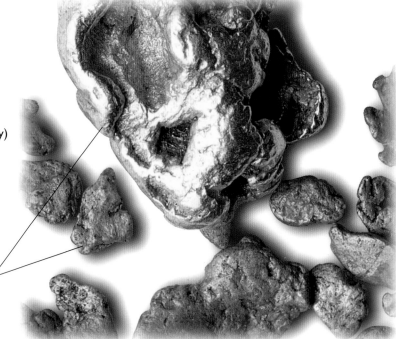

A gold nugget and flakes. Each flake is about 3 mm long.

Graphite

Carbon C

Colour: Grey-black and shiny
Streak: Grey-black
Hardness: 2
Cleavage: Perfect to form thin flakes
Crystals: Hexagonal
Other: Specific gravity about 2

Graphite is a black, soft form of carbon, harder than coal, but far softer than diamond. The name comes from the Greek *graphein*, meaning to write. Graphite naturally crumbles to release tiny flakes. This occurs because, in graphite, the carbon atoms are arranged in sheets that are poorly linked to each other. As a result, one sheet of crystals readily slides over another.

Graphite is formed by the metamorphic change of coal and other carbon-containing materials that were originally formed in sedimentary rocks. It is commonly found in schists and in marble.

Graphite

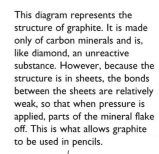

Platinum

Platinum Pt

Colour: Tin-white to grey. Does not tarnish
Hardness: 4
Cleavage: None
Crystals: Cubic
Streak: Light grey
Other: Specific gravity 14–19, a very heavy metal.

The name platinum is taken from the Spanish *plata*, meaning silver. Platinum is one of the group of elements called heavy metals, and that is the best way of identifying it.

Platinum is formed in deep-seated, intrusive, igneous rocks, but it is rarely found in this form. Equally rare are nuggets, or any other substantial piece of metal. Nonetheless, this does not mean that platinum is rare. In fact, it is very widely distributed around the world, mostly in placer deposits.

This diagram represents the structure of graphite. It is made only of carbon minerals and is, like diamond, an unreactive substance. However, because the structure is in sheets, the bonds between the sheets are relatively weak, so that when pressure is applied, parts of the mineral flake off. This is what allows graphite to be used in pencils.

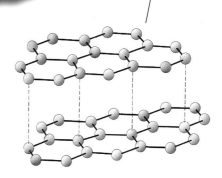

Silver

Silver Ag

Colour: Silver-white, tarnishes
to brown and black
Streak: Light grey
Hardness: 3
Cleavage: None
Crystals: Cubic
Other: Specific gravity 10–11, very heavy metal.

Silver has been sought after since the earliest
times and is regarded as a precious metal, just as
gems are precious stones. Silver is often found in
veins that were once close to magma chambers,
alongside gold and copper.

Dendritic silver. Native silver,
which is tarnishing grey on
exposure to the air, set in a
mineral groundmass.

Sulphur

Sulphur S

Colour: Primrose yellow or amber
Streak: White
Hardness: 2
Cleavage: Poor
Crystals: Orthorhombic
Other: Specific gravity 2, a lightweight substance.

Sulphur is a non-metal. It can form crystals in
more than one crystal system.

Sulphur produces bright yellow crystals in
the monoclinic system (where crystals look like
double-ended chisel blades) and amber crystals
in the rhombic system (where crystals look like
three-dimensional parallelograms, like a
matchbox whose base has been fixed while
its top has been pushed sideways).

Most sulphur is formed directly by
deposition from volcanic gases and so
commonly occurs in volcanic rocks.

Sulphur crystals form in two of the
crystal systems, monoclinic and rhombic.
Those to the right and above are rhombic
crystals of sulphur. Another way to identify
them is by their colour: rhombic crystals
have an amber colouring; monoclinic crystals
(such as those on the right) are bright yellow.

This sulphur deposit
from Poland shows a
clear crystal structure.

Sulphur

Sulphides

Sulphides are simple compounds containing metallic elements and sulphur. Most sulphides are soft, heavy and brittle and have a metallic lustre (hence pyrite – iron pyrite, or iron sulphide, is called 'fool's gold'). Most sulphides are opaque and have bright colours and coloured streaks. Metals found in sulphides include iron, copper, zinc, lead, cobalt, nickel, silver, and mercury. Not surprisingly, sulphides are the major ores of many metals, including copper, zinc, lead, silver, and mercury.

Sulphides are not stable when exposed to the air, and weather readily. Some are also soluble in water.

Most sulphides are heavy because they contain metal atoms.

Some granites contain large numbers of small veins containing sulphides. Copper sulphide is the most common mineral in these deposits. They are porphyritic rocks, meaning they contain large crystals. Their location has given rise to some of the world's largest mines, for example, the porphyry coppers of the western United States at Bingham, Utah. The molybdenum deposit at Climax, Colorado, near Leadville is also a porphyry in granite.

In some cases sulphides have separated out from the cooling magma to form very concentrated deposits. Examples include the copper and nickel deposits at Sudbury, Ontario, Canada.

There are several hundred sulphides. Here are some of the common ones:

(Below) Pyrite 'dollar' in shale.

Bornite

Copper iron sulphide Cu_5FeS_4

Colour: Copper-red when fresh but usually seen as the tarnished form, which is deep blue, hence the name of the ore is peacock ore.

Hardness: 3

Cleavage: None

Crystals: Cubic

Streak: Grey-black

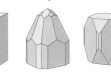

Other: Specific gravity 5, a moderately heavy mineral.

Bornite and chalcopyrite are minerals containing both copper and iron sulphides. They are the source of half of the world's copper ores.

Chalcopyrite (see below) is a brassy-coloured mineral, while bornite is often a rich peacock-blue (in fact, it is often called peacock ore). They are hydrothermal replacement minerals. The sample shown here is made mainly of bornite; but, if you look closely, you will see the gold speckles of chalcopyrite as well. Bornite is named after the Austrian geologist, Ignaz von Born.

Bornite

Chalcopyrite

Copper iron sulphide ore $CuFeS_2$

Colour: Brassy yellow that tarnishes to deep blue

Hardness: 4

Cleavage: Poor

Crystals: Tetragonal

Streak: Greenish black

Other: Specific gravity 4; slightly above average; brittle mineral. Another mineral (along with pyrite) that is sometimes mistaken for gold. It is one of the main ores of copper; often found in the same deposits as bornite and pyrite. Chalcopyrite comes from the Greek *chalos*, meaning copper, and *pyrites*, meaning fire.

Chalcopyrite

Galena

Lead sulphide PbS

Colour: Dark lead-grey. Does not tarnish

Hardness: 3

Cleavage: Perfect three directions

Crystals: Cubic

Streak: Dark grey

Other: Specific gravity 7.5, a heavy mineral.

Lead sulphide has the same kind of structure as salt, having equal numbers of lead and sulphur atoms. This makes its crystals part of the cubic system. Thus, it has some of the features of a metal, being bright and shiny, but others of a non-metal, and, like salt, it is brittle.

Galena is found in places that have experienced volcanic activity. It is associated with zones from which

Galena, lead sulphide

miners collect other ores, such as silver and tin.

It is also found in limestone and dolomite rocks through which heated waters have passed – that is, it can be a hydrothermal mineral. Galena comes from the Greek *galena*, meaning lead ore.

Pyrite can sometimes appear almost silvery.

Molybdenite

Molybdenum sulphide MoS_2

Colour: Bluish lead-grey

Hardness: 1

Cleavage: Perfect into sheets

Crystals: Hexagonal

Streak: Grey-black

Other: Specific gravity 5, a moderately heavy mineral; feels greasy; can be confused with graphite, but graphite is blacker. Occurs as thin sheets (scales).

This mineral is found in hydrothermal metamorphic rocks, along with quartz, cassiterite, and chalcopyrite.

Molybdenum comes from the Greek *molybdos*, meaning lead. Molybdenite is the most important ore of molybdenum.

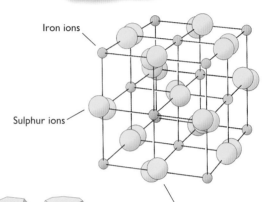

Iron ions

Sulphur ions

Pyrite

Iron sulphide FeS_2

Colour: Pale or brassy yellow (hence fool's gold)

Hardness: 6

Cleavage: None

Crystals: Cubic with **STRIATIONS** on the faces

Streak: Greenish black

Other: Specific gravity 5; pyrite produces sparks when struck against a steel penknife blade. Is sometimes mistaken for gold. Often found in the same deposits as bornite.

Iron sulphide has two sulphide atoms for every one iron atom. It is a bright, brassy colour (sometimes mistaken for gold, hence the name 'fool's gold'). Pyrite is, however, much less dense than gold, and much harder. The darker form of pyrite is called marcasite.

Pyrite is found abundantly in connection with hot volcanic waters on the ocean floor, but is also formed as a hydrothermal replacement deposit.

Shale rocks contain pyrite because the muds from which they are formed were once also combined with decaying organic matter. As the organic matter decayed, it took oxygen from the water, and hydrogen sulphide gas was produced. The hydrogen sulphide reacted with iron in the water to produce iron sulphide. In the right conditions the iron sulphide grew into perfect cubic

In a pyrite cube an iron ion occurs at each corner of the cube and in the middle of each of the faces. A pair of sulphur ions are found half-way along each edge.

crystals; in other circumstances it developed into nodules; and in rarer situations it developed into pyrite 'dollars' (see page 35).

Iron sulphide is not stable in damp air, where it readily reacts with oxygen so that the bright surface of a newly exposed pyrite quickly becomes dull and then changes to a fine grey powder. Pyrite comes from the Greek *pyr*, meaning fire.

Sphalerite

Zinc sulphide ZnS
Colour: Yellow, red-brown or green and looks resinous
Hardness: 4
Cleavage: Perfect six directions
Crystals: Cubic
Streak: Light brown
Other: Specific gravity 14–19, a very heavy mineral.

Although at first glance it appears black, careful inspection reveals that this sphalerite sample is a deep, resinous yellow.

Zinc sulphide has four sulphur atoms surrounding each zinc atom, and four zinc atoms surrounding each sulphur atom. Pure sphalerite is colourless, the colours being given to the mineral by iron impurities; with increasing iron the colours change to green, brown, red, and black. Red to yellow-coloured sphalerite does not look like a metal, being transparent or translucent and looking something like dull amber. Black sphalerite looks more metallic. Sphalerite containing cadmium is bright orange.

Zinc is found among many other metals in hydrothermal replacement deposits.

Zinc sulphide is the most abundant and important zinc mineral. It is also called zinc blende. Sphalerite comes from the Greek *sphaleros*, meaning treacherous.

Stibnite

Antimony trisulphide Sb_2S_3
Colour: Lead-grey
Hardness: 2
Cleavage: Perfect one direction
Crystals: Orthorhombic
Streak: Dark lead grey
Other: Specific gravity 4.6; crystals striated along their length. Crystals will bend slightly without breaking. Many crystals are bent and twisted.

This mineral is found in hydrothermal veins.

Stibnite comes from the Greek word *stibi*, meaning antimony. Stibnite is the most common ore of antimony.

Stibnite

Oxides

Oxide minerals consist of oxygen bonded to one or more metal atoms (but note that silicon dioxide, quartz, is called a silicate, not an oxide).

Oxide minerals are hard and dense. They are often strongly coloured, fairly unreactive, and so insoluble. Oxides are found in all types of rock. They form crystals and nodules in igneous rocks and some metamorphic rocks, and coatings and granules in sedimentary rocks.

The most common oxides are haematite, magnetite (both iron oxides), and rutile (titanium oxide). Other important oxides are chromite (chromium oxide), spinel (magnesium aluminium oxide), corundum (aluminium oxide), cassiterite (tin oxide) and pyrolusite (manganese oxide).

Hydroxides are a combination of oxygen and hydrogen with one or more metal atoms. These minerals are softer than oxides. Most of them represent the result of weathering. The most important hydroxide minerals are bauxite (aluminium hydroxide), and goethite (iron hydroxide).

Bauxite

Hydrated aluminium oxide (gibbsite $Al(OH)_3$)
Colour: White, but often associated with iron oxides and, therefore, appears orange.
Hardness: 2
Cleavage: None
Crystals: None. Massive but normally found as granules (called pisoliths)
Streak: White
Other: Specific gravity 4

It is a weathered product of surface processes and is always found close to the ground surface, not in rocks.

Bauxite is named after Les Baux, a small place in southern France. It is the main ore of aluminium.

Chromite

Iron chromium oxide $FeCr_2O_4$
Colour: Black
Hardness: 5
Cleavage: None
Crystals: Cubic
Streak: Dark brown
Other: Specific gravity 4.3–5.0; it is weakly magnetic. It is formed in many basic igneous rocks.

Chromium comes from the Greek *chroma*, meaning colour. Chromium minerals are often brightly coloured when refined.

Chromite

Bauxite

Cassiterite

Tin oxide SnO_2. One of the main ores of tin; found in hydrothermal veins.

Colour: Brown to black
Hardness: 6
Cleavage: Distinct
Crystals: Tetragonal, usually as twinned crystals
Streak: Light brown
Other: Specific gravity 7; heavy mineral. The most common tin-bearing mineral.

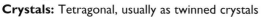

The word cassiterite comes from the Greek word *kassiteros*, meaning tin.

Cassiterite

Goethite

Hydrated iron(III) oxide $Fe_2O_3 \cdot H_2O$.

Colour: Yellowish brown
Hardness: 5
Cleavage: Perfect
Crystals: Orthorhombic
Streak: Yellow
Other: Specific gravity 3.3–4.3

It is a secondary iron mineral often associated with alteration of hydrothermal iron minerals.

Goethite is named after Goethe, the German poet, who was also an amateur mineralogist.

Corundum

Corundum

Aluminium oxide Al_2O_3

Colour: White to grey and light brown, as well as nearly black, but when coloured deep red, it is called ruby; when blue, green and other colours, it is called sapphire. It is also black.
Hardness: 9
Cleavage: None, fracture conchoidal
Crystals: Hexagonal
Streak: White
Other: Specific gravity 4; slightly above average; brittle mineral; hardness only second to diamond.

It is found in metamorphic rocks, such as gneiss and hornfels, syenite pegmatites. The name corundum comes from *kuruvinda*, a Sanskrit word for ruby. The world's best rubies come from Myanmar (Burma), where they have been naturally weathered from rocks and washed by rivers to accumulate among river gravels.

Ruby

Haematite

Iron oxide Fe_2O_3. One of the main ores of iron; found in igneous, metamorphic, and sedimentary rocks.

Colour: Steel-grey on fresh face and reddish-brown when tarnished

Hardness: 6

Cleavage: None, fracture splintery

Crystals: Hexagonal

Streak: Red

Other: Specific gravity 5; slightly above average; brittle mineral.

Pure iron forms the grey coloured crystals.

The word haematite comes from the Greek *haimatites*, meaning colour of blood. Haematite is the most widespread form of iron ore. It is found in sedimentary rocks. The iron oxide colour is deep red. Haematite was formed in tropical regions with wet and dry seasons. During the wet season, the minerals eroded from the land were washed to basins, deltas, or coasts. During the dry period, the water evaporated, the sediments dried out, and the iron compounds oxidised to iron oxide. These rocks are often referred to as 'red beds'.

A piece of iron ore (haematite). The deep red colour is due to the fact that haematite is iron oxide.

Ilmenite

Iron titanium oxide $FeTiO_3$

Colour: Brownish-black, metallic lustre

Hardness: 5

Cleavage: None

Crystals: Hexagonal

Streak: Black

Other: Specific gravity 5; slightly above average; brittle mineral.

The word Ilmenite comes from the place where it was found, the Ilmen Mountains in Russia. One of the main ores of titanium; found in igneous, metamorphic, and sedimentary rocks. Mostly obtained from placer mining.

Limonite

Hydrated iron(III) oxide $Fe_2O_3 \cdot H_2O$

Colour: Yellow

Hardness: 5

Cleavage: None

Crystals: None. Amorphous mixture of iron oxides

Streak: Yellowish brown

Other: Specific gravity 2.7–4.3 depending on water content.

It is a secondary iron mineral.

Limonite is named after the Greek *leimons*, meaning meadow.

Limonite is an iron oxide that forms in cooler climates than haematite. It is usually yellow, orange, and brown, rather than red. It contains water molecules and so is an example of a hydrous (water-containing) iron oxide.

Limonite is often found in marshes and is, thus, also known as bog iron ore.

Steel grey faces of haematite.

Magnetite

Iron oxide Fe_3O_4
Colour: Black
Hardness: 6
Cleavage: None
Crystals: Cubic
Streak: Black

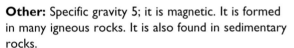

Other: Specific gravity 5; it is magnetic. It is formed in many igneous rocks. It is also found in sedimentary rocks.

Magnetite was named after Magnesia, an ancient name for a district near Macedonia in Eastern Europe.

Magnetite is also known as lodestone. The magnetic property is created because each tiny crystal of iron can behave as a magnet, organising itself into the same direction as all those crystals nearby. Magnetite is associated with regional metamorphic rocks.

This piece of magnetite has been dipped in iron filings to demonstrate its magnetic properties.

Pyrolusite

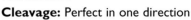

Manganese dioxide MnO_2
Colour: Black
Hardness: 5
Cleavage: Perfect in one direction
Crystals: Tetragonal, usually as massive columns
Streak: Sooty black
Other: Specific gravity 4.4–5.0; slightly above average; powdery black mineral

The word pyrolusite comes from the Greek *pyr*, meaning fire, and *louein*, to wash. It was used in glass-making to get rid of (wash out) the iron contamination that otherwise gives glass a greenish tinge. One of the main ores of manganese; found in hydrothermal veins.

Rutile

Titanium dioxide TiO_2
Colour: Reddish, striated (lined) crystals
Hardness: 6
Cleavage: Distinct
Crystals: Tetragonal
Streak: White
Other: Specific gravity 4.3; slightly above average; brittle mineral.

The word rutile comes from the Latin word *rutilus*, meaning red-coloured.

Rutile is found in igneous, metamorphic rocks. Mostly obtained from blue schists and in hydrothermal veins. Original environment of formation is gabbro, an alkaline plutonic rock, and in dykes. Rutile is the main ore of titanium and also used for gemstones.

Uraninite

Uranium oxide UO_2
Colour: Green to brownish black
Hardness: 5
Cleavage: None

Crystals: Tetragonal, usually as twinned crystals
Streak: Light brown
Other: Specific gravity 6.5–10, heavy mineral.

One of the main ores of uranium; found in hydrothermal veins. It is the most common uranium-bearing mineral. Normally surrounded by brightly coloured alteration products.

The word uraninite comes from the name of the element uranium.

Halides

Halides are compounds that contain a halogen (chlorine, fluorine, iodine, or bromine) ion in the mineral. The halides are soft and brittle, and most dissolve easily.

Halides are found in tiny amounts in all the freshwater rivers and lakes of the world. But if the water dries out, the halides are left behind, leaving 'salt' deposits. The most common is sodium chloride, also called common salt, or rock salt.

Considerable thicknesses of salt deposits are common in most deserts and also in salt marshes near estuaries.

Halite

Sodium chloride NaCl
Colour: Colourless
Hardness: 2
Cleavage: Perfect
Crystals: Cubic
Streak: White

Other: Specific gravity 2.2; its tastes salty. It is also found in sedimentary rocks as beds of evaporites representing ancient lake beds or lagoons. Vitreous lustre.

The name halite comes from the Greek word *hals*, meaning salt.

Crystals of salt are soft and easily scratched. They are mostly white, although they may be tinged with orange if they have some iron staining.

Fluorite

Calcium fluoride CaF$_2$
Colour: Violet, blue, and yellow
Hardness: 4
Cleavage: Perfect, producing cubes and octahedron
Crystals: Cubic
Streak: White
Other: Specific gravity 3.0; transparent or translucent crystals. Twins common. It is found in hydrothermal deposits.

The name fluorite comes from the Latin word *fluere*, meaning to flow. That is because fluorite was used as a flux in smelting ores, because it melts easily and flows into gaps.

Cubic fluorite

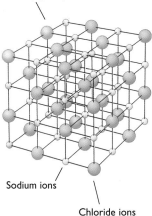

Halite contains sodium and chloride ions formed in a regular cubic framework (see also page 18).

Sodium ions

Chloride ions

Carbonates

Carbonate minerals are easily identified because they fizz when acid is dropped onto them. Calcite and dolomite are the most important carbonate minerals. Other important carbonates are malachite and azurite, which are both copper ores. They can be found in both hydrothermal and sedimentary rocks. Carbonates are among the most common minerals in rocks. Most carbonates are white, colourless or transparent. Many carbonates are brittle and readily fracture into rhombohedral-shaped pieces. Calcite is the main mineral in all limestones and chalks. Calcite is also widely found in hydrothermal deposits.

Aragonite

Calcium carbonate $CaCO_3$
Colour: White, colourless, pale grey
Hardness: 4
Cleavage: Good in one direction, poor in two others
Crystals: Orthorhombic
Streak: White
Other: Specific gravity 2.9–3.0; effervesces in acid; radial habit and hexagonal-looking prismatic crystals. Almost always twinned.

Aragonite is named after Aragon province in Spain, where it was found. Aragonite is not as common as calcite and tends to form in evaporite deposits. Sometimes found in hydrothermal deposits.

Twinned crystals of aragonite.

Azurite

Copper carbonate $Cu_3(CO_3)_2(OH)_2$
Colour: Azure blue
Hardness: 4
Cleavage: Good in two directions, fracture conchoidal
Crystals: Monoclinic, many crystals are tabular; also occurs in nodules.
Streak: Blue
Other: Specific gravity 3.8

A secondary copper mineral that develops in hydrothermal deposits as they are altered over time. Often found with malachite.

Azurite is named after the colour of the mineral.

Azurite

Calcite

Calcium carbonate $CaCO_3$
Colour: White, colourless, pale grey
Hardness: 3
Cleavage: Perfect in three directions to produce rhombohedra
Crystals: Hexagonal
Streak: White
Other: Specific gravity 2.7; effervesces in acid; looking through a transparent crystal produces two images.

Calcite is named after the Greek word *chalx*, meaning lime.

Calcite often forms in rhombohedral-shaped crystals. The faces are parallelograms.

Dolomite

Calcium magnesium carbonate $CaMg(CO_3)_2$

Colour: White, colourless, pale pink

Hardness: 4

Cleavage: Perfect in three directions to make rhombohedra

Crystals: Hexagonal

Streak: White

Other: Specific gravity 2.8; effervesces in acid. Faces are curved, not flat.

Dolomite is named after the 18th-century French mineralogist Deodat de Dolomieu.

Dolomite (white) with pyrite (yellow) crystals

Malachite

Copper carbonate $Cu_2CO_3(OH)_2$

Colour: Green

Hardness: 4

Cleavage: Perfect in one direction, fracture conchoidal

Crystals: Monoclinic

Streak: Green

Other: Specific gravity 4; often shows concentric colour banding; rare as crystals but usually as nodules.

A secondary copper mineral that develops in hydrothermal deposits as they are altered over time. Often found with azurite.

Malachite is named after the Greek word *moloche*, meaning mallow, because the mallow has leaves of a green colour similar to that of malachite.

Malachite

Borates

An uncommon group of minerals. The main borate mineral is borax.

Borax

Hydrous sodium borate $Na_2B_4O_7 \cdot 10H_2O$

Colour: White, colourless

Hardness: 2

Cleavage: Perfect in one direction, fracture conchoidal

Crystals: Monoclinic

Streak: White

Other: Specific gravity 1.7; a light mineral. Dissolves in water.

It is an evaporite mineral that formed in desert lakes. An uncommon mineral but historically well known because of the borax mines in Death Valley, California, USA, and the 20 mule teams that had to pull the mineral from the mines through the searing heat of the desert summer.

Borax is derived from the Arabic word *buraq*, meaning borax.

Sulphates

Sulphate minerals have a metal ion combined with a sulphate ion. They vary greatly in their properties. Most are lightweight and brittle.

Anhydrite

Calcium sulphate $CaSO_4$

Colour: White

Hardness: 2

Cleavage: Good three directions; fracture uneven

Crystals: Orthorhombic, but crystals are rare

Streak: White

Other: Specific gravity 3.0. Anhydrite is mainly found as massive white deposits. It is often transparent to translucent.

The name anhydrite is derived from the Greek meaning 'without water'.

It is mainly an evaporite deposit and forms together with gypsum and halite.

Barite

Barium sulphate $BaSO_4$.

Colour: Steel grey on fresh face and reddish-brown when tarnished

Hardness: 3

Cleavage: Perfect in one direction

Crystals: Orthorhombic, but usually in the form of tabular crystals.

Streak: White

Other: Specific gravity 4.3–4.6. Feels heavy for a white, non-metallic mineral, and this is its best distinguishing characteristic.

The word barite comes from the Greek *barys* meaning 'heavy'. It occurs in hydrothermal deposits.

Barite

Gypsum

Hydrous calcium sulphate $CaSO_4 \cdot 2H_2O$. It occurs in hydrothermal and evaporite deposits.

Colour: White

Hardness: 2

Cleavage: Good in three directions, fracture uneven

Crystals: Monoclinic, but usually in the form of tabular crystals.

Streak: White

Other: Specific gravity 3.0. Usually occurs in massive pieces, and crystals are rare. It is an important evaporite mineral formed in desert lakes and lagoons.

The word gypsum comes from the Greek word *gypsos*, meaning 'chalk'.

These are desert roses, made from calcium sulphate, or gypsum. The crystals of this mineral look a bit like rose petals, hence its name. The monoclinic crystals give it a look different from the more block-like cubic crystals of pyrite.

Chromates

Chromate minerals are not common. They contain a metal linked to a chromate ion. They are mainly very brightly coloured.

Phosphates

A rare group of minerals of which apatite is the most common.

Apatite

Calcium phosphate $Ca_5(PO_4)_3$

Colour: Green to brown

Hardness: 5

Cleavage: Poor, fracture uneven

Crystals: Hexagonal, mostly in the form of short prisms.

Streak: White

Other: Specific gravity 3. Apatite is the only common phosphate mineral. It forms in igneous rocks.

Apatite is named after the Greek word *apate*, meaning 'deceit' because it is easily confused with many other minerals.

A prism of apatite

Silicates

Silicates are minerals that are combinations of silicon and oxygen with metal ions. Silicate minerals are found in nearly all rocks.

There are more than a thousand silicate minerals known. For example, emerald, aquamarine, citrine, tourmaline, topaz, agate, jasper and chalcedony are all silicates.

Silicates occur in about one-third of the minerals in the earth's crust, making up about 93% of the earth's crust by volume and about 75% of the earth's crust by weight.

Although there are so many different minerals in this group, they share many common characteristics. In general, most silicates are hard and do not dissolve in water; most do not even dissolve in acids. This is one reason why many rocks so are resistant to weathering. When they do weather, they form more silicates, usually clay minerals.

The crystals of silicate minerals tend to look glassy, and most of the crystals are transparent or translucent.

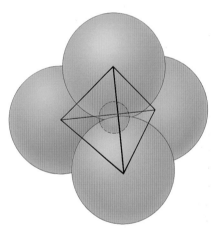

(Above) This diagram represents a silica unit. It is in the form of a four-cornered solid called a tetrahedron, with a small silicon atom surrounded by four oxygen atoms. It is the basic building block of all the silicate minerals.

The molecules build up in frameworks, with every oxygen atom being shared between two tetrahedra. Most other framework silicates contain some aluminium substituting for silicon, and also calcium, sodium, or potassium. Minerals include the feldspars.

Silicate groups

The variety in silicates is accounted for by the way the silica units can group, or cluster, together into chains, rings, sheets, and framework patterns. That is the basis of how silicates are classified.

Framework silicates

The simplest structure of a silicate, which we know as the mineral quartz, is the most abundant of all minerals. It is very stable, consisting of a silicon atom surrounded by four oxygen atoms. The shape these atoms make is called a tetrahedron.

Quartz

Silicon dioxide SiO_2

Colour: Colourless, white and many colours if containing impurities. Rock crystal contains no impurities and is colourless; amethyst is purple; rose quartz is pink to red (see page 22); citrine is yellow-brown; smoky quartz is dark brown or grey; milky quartz is white

Hardness: 7

Cleavage: None; conchoidal fracture

Crystals: Hexagonal usually as prisms

Streak: White

Other: Specific gravity 2.7. A widespread and important mineral in all igneous rocks, but especially so in acidic rocks, such as granite. It makes up much of sandstone, the quartz grains being originally weathered out of granites.

The word quartz has a German origin that has been lost.

Quartz is also known as 'rock crystal'. Quartz is an example of a mineral made of silica molecules that extend outward in every direction to make a framework. No other elements are involved in building the frame. This makes quartz a particularly stable mineral. Quartz is also common as non-crystalline silica filling in veins and other fractures in rock.

Coloured quartz is known by a variety of names. Violet-coloured quartz is called amethyst, dark brown or grey quartz is smoky quartz, and yellow-brown coloured quartz is called citrine.

In these crystals of quartz the hexagonal (six-sided) crystals can be seen. These crystals are about six centimetres long; some quartz crystals grow to a huge size and can weigh several tonnes.

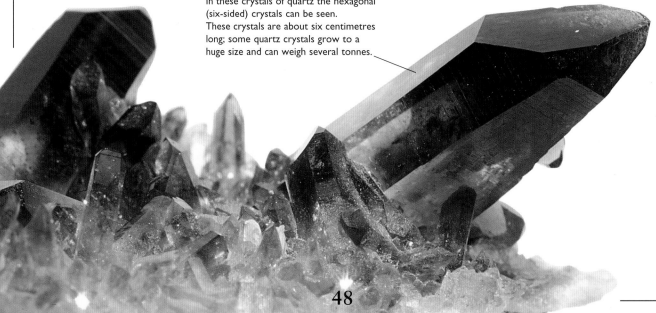

A geode into which quartz crystals have grown

Amethyst (below) is a form of quartz that has been contaminated with iron, manganese, and carbon and has taken on a violet hue. It changes to yellow-brown citrine (right) on heating.

Chalcedony, Agate, Jasper

Silicon dioxide SiO_2. Essentially quartz with iron and aluminium that produces the characteristic coloured bands

Colour: White or grey, but with impurities: carnelian red or brownish-red; onyx: brownish-red carnelian in layers; bloodstone: bright green with red spots; agate: banded red and brown; jasper: mottled reds and yellows with brown; flint: white or grey to black; cat's eye contains asbestos

Hardness: 7

Cleavage: None; conchoidal fracture

Crystals: None

Streak: White

Other: Specific gravity 2.7. A widespread and important mineral that can form in hydrothermal alteration zones near magma bodies, and also as nodules by precipitation (flint). Chalcedony in the form of agate is the mineral that replaces many trees to make petrified forests; circular-banded agates are found as **AMYGDULES** in basalt.

The word chalcedony comes from Chalcedon, an ancient Greek city.

These banded forms of silica are considered to be gemstones. They enter cavities inside rocks as silica-rich solutions. These then cool, and the silica is precipitated on the inside of the cavity. Typically, such cavities form inside lavas and other igneous rocks when they are cooling. Jasper (red), chalcedony (grey), and carnelian (red) are all forms of the same kind of deposition.

Cat's-eye gets its name from the luminous, reflective bands that resemble the slit pupil of a cat. Although it is predominantly silica, the reflective area contains asbestos fibres and the green colour comes from the copper oxides in the silica structure.

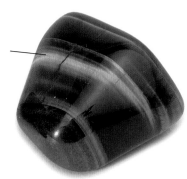

Opal

Hydrous silicon dioxide $SiO_2 \cdot nH_2O$. Essentially quartz with water in the structure

Colour: White, yellow, red and brown; the way the light is reflected internally is called opalescence.

Hardness: 6

Cleavage: None; conchoidal fracture

Crystals: None

Streak: White

Other: Specific gravity 2.7. Develops as cavity infillings (**VUGS**). It is also found replacing shells of fossil molluscs and trees.

The word opal comes from the Sanskrit word *upala*, meaning 'precious stone'. Opal has no crystals at all. It forms as a precipitate from a solution of water containing silica. In fact, opal stones contain water molecules. As a result, it is less dense than other forms of quartz. Opal also has a lustre different from other forms of quartz, being more like that of a pearl.

Feldspars

Feldspar minerals are found in most igneous rocks. They are silicates in which some of the silicon atoms have been replaced by aluminium atoms. When this happens, however, some 'holes' are left in the structure, allowing a range of metal atoms, such as potassium, sodium or calcium, to fit in. This is what produces the variety in feldspars.

Feldspar crystals are mainly opaque and either pink, grey or white. Translucent examples include labradorite.

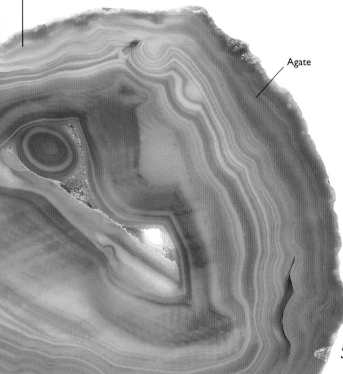

Agate

Orthoclase (feldspar)
also called potash feldspar

Potassium aluminium silicate $KAlSi_3O_8$

Colour: White or grey, sometimes pink

Hardness: 6

Cleavage: Good

Crystals: Monoclinic, mainly occurs as prismatic square-sectioned crystals

Streak: White

Other: Specific gravity 2.5–2.6. A common mineral in granite and other acidic plutonic rocks.

The word orthoclase comes from the Greek words *orthos*, meaning 'upright' and *klaiss*, meaning 'fracture'.

Orthoclase
feldspar

Plagioclase (feldspar)

(also called soda-lime feldspars and lime-soda feldspars)

Sodium or calcium aluminium silicate, for example, $NaAlSi_3O_8$ and $CaAl_2Si_2O_8$

Colour: White or grey

Hardness: 6

Cleavage: Good

Crystals: Triclinic. Often forms twins that look like plate-like crystals stacked up

Streak: White

Other: Specific gravity 2.7. A common mineral in granite and other acidic plutonic rocks. The crystals have tiny parallel 'scratch-marks' (striations) on the surface. Microcline is similar. It normally forms the matrix in which 'graphic granite' quartz crystals occur.

Plagioclase
feldspar

(Below) Labradorite: a translucent plagioclase feldspar, whose name is taken from the first place it was found, Labrador, Canada.

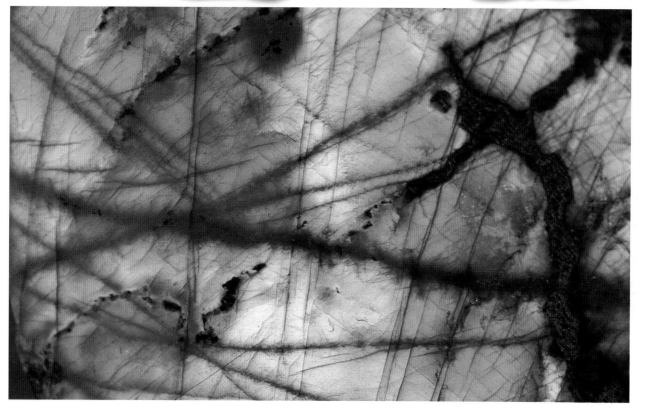

Zeolites

Zeolites are a group of water-absorbing silicates related to feldspars. They are most common in cavities in basic igneous rocks. Their structure has water inside the aluminium silicate structure.

Orthosilicates

In these silicates, the silica molecules are held together by metal atoms. This influences the shape of the crystals in each mineral.

The minerals in this group form at very high temperatures and are only in rocks associated with volcanoes and mountain building. Two of the more easily recognised are garnet and zircon. However, the most widespread of these minerals is olivine.

Andalusite

Aluminium silicate Al_2SiO_5
Colour: White, grey
Hardness: 7
Cleavage: Good, two directions
Crystals: Orthorhombic, found mainly as small columnar crystals
Streak: Colourless
Other: Specific gravity 3.2. A common mineral metamorphic rocks and also in granites.

Andalusite is named after the region of Andalusia in Spain.

Garnet

A group name for calcium and aluminium silicates such as $Ca_3Al_2Si_3O_{12}$ – known as grossular – and $Fe_3Al_2Si_3O_{12}$ – known as almandine.
Colour: Deep red to brownish-red (in almandine), also pale green (in grossular)
Hardness: 7
Cleavage: None
Crystals: Cubic, found frequently as crystals of dodecahedral shape
Streak: Colourless
Other: Specific gravity 3.5–4.3. A common mineral in metamorphic rocks, especially schists (garnetiferous mica-schists).

Almandine is named after the place Alabanda; grossular after Latin word *grossularia*, meaning

Garnet

'gooseberry' because of the pale green colour.

Garnets are combinations of iron and silica with calcium, aluminium and manganese. The metals are responsible for the variety of colours.

Garnets are all hard and have a glassy lustre. Some are formed in granites but are especially common in metamorphic rocks such as schist, where they form crystals that are much harder than the surrounding rock. Weathering of rocks makes the garnets protrude and become easy to spot.

Kyanite

Aluminium silicate Al_2SiO_5

Colour: Light blue to grey, translucent

Hardness: 7 lengthwise; 4 crosswise

Cleavage: Perfect one direction lengthwise

Crystals: Triclinic as bladed crystals

Streak: Colourless

Other: Specific gravity 3.6. Found in regional metamorphic rocks such as gneiss and schist.

Kyanite can form beautiful blue blade-shaped crystals and is one of the major mineral resources of India.

The name kyanite comes from the Greek word *kyanos*, meaning 'dark blue'.

Kyanite is formed during the regional metamorphism of clay-rich sediments that have been deeply buried and subjected to heat, rather than pressure. Kyanite occurs as elongated blades mainly in gneisses and schists.

Olivine

Magnesium iron silicate $(Mg,Fe)_2SiO_4$

Colour: Olive-green, yellowish-green (when transparent it is called peridot)

Hardness: 7

Cleavage: Indistinct

Crystals: Orthorhombic, found mainly as grains not crystals

Streak: Colourless

Other: Specific gravity 3.2–4.3. A common mineral in volcanic and plutonic basic rocks, such as gabbro and basalt, where it is an essential mineral.

The name olivine comes from its olive-green colour. Olivines are greenish minerals found in many igneous rocks.

They are minerals associated with very high temperature and pressure, and are more common in rocks that have been made from materials deep within the earth. The diamond pipes of Kimberley, South Africa, consist mainly of olivine.

Olivine

Staurolite

Iron and aluminium silicate $Fe_2Al_9Si_4O_{22}(OH)_2$

Colour: Yellowish-brown

Hardness: 7

Cleavage: Poor

Crystals: Monoclinic, often as cross-twinned crystals

Streak: White

Other: Specific gravity 3.7. Found in regional metamorphic rocks.

The name staurolite comes from the Greek word *stauros*, meaning 'cross'.

Topaz

Zircon

Zirconium silicate $ZrSiO_4$

Colour: Brown, grey, transparent (when known as hyacinth), smoky (when known as jargoon)

Hardness: 7

Cleavage: Indistinct

Crystals: Tetragonal; often as square-sectioned prisms

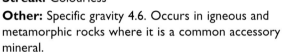

Streak: Colourless

Other: Specific gravity 4.6. Occurs in igneous and metamorphic rocks where it is a common accessory mineral.

The name zircon is from the Persian word *zargun*, meaning 'gold-coloured'. Zircon can be cut into brilliant sparkling, diamond-like crystals. In nature it often forms pyramid-headed crystals. Zircon can be found as tiny crystals in many igneous rocks, where it may vary in colour from brown to green or be colourless. Zircon is very resistant to weathering and so is also found in sediments, such as sandstone, where it often makes up dark grains among the pale grains of quartz.

The transparent form is called 'Matura diamond'. It has a structure of atoms similar to real diamond. Synthetic zircon is used in jewellery as a substitute for diamonds (known commonly as CZs – pronounced 'ceezees' – cubic zirconia).

Zircon

Topaz

Aluminium fluorsilicate $Al_2SiO_4(F,OH)_2$

Colour: White, colourless (when it is a gemstone), green

Hardness: 8

Cleavage: Perfect, one direction

Crystals: Orthorhombic, found mainly as short prismatic crystals or in massive form

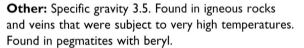

Streak: Colourless

Other: Specific gravity 3.5. Found in igneous rocks and veins that were subject to very high temperatures. Found in pegmatites with beryl.

The name topaz is from the Greek word *topazos*, meaning 'unknown gemstone' because it was unknown to ancient civilisations.

Topaz is regarded as a gemstone. It is an aluminium silicate containing fluorine. It forms from fluorine-bearing vapours in hydrothermal environments and is found in cavities in lava, granite, dykes, and veins. It often occurs in association with tin ore (cassiterite) and is used to help in prospecting for tin. Pure topaz produces a brilliant cut and can look like a diamond. Coloured topaz can also be found, but the colour often fades in sunlight. Pink topaz is yellow topaz that has been heat treated artificially and is called Brazilian ruby. A deeper red topaz also occurs naturally.

Ring silicates

Silica molecules can form into rings, usually in groups of six. The most common form is called beryl, and the gemstone forms are emerald and aquamarine.

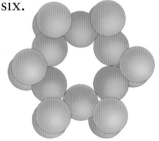

Beryl

Beryllium aluminium silicate $Be_3Al_2Si_6O_{18}$

Colour: Green (when it is transparent, it is called emerald); blue (when it is transparent, it is called aquamarine).

Hardness: 8

Cleavage: Indistinct, one direction

Crystals: Hexagonal, mostly as prisms

Streak: Colourless

Other: Specific gravity 2.7 to 2.9. Found in pegmatites and in schists.

Beryl

The name beryl is from the Greek word *beryllos*, meaning a 'green gem'. The glassy-green mineral is often found in large pieces, sometimes several metres long. They are formed by rings of six silica molecules stacked one above the other in sheets. Beryllium atoms help hold the sheets together.

Beryl is commonly found in granites, along with tourmaline.

Emerald

Aquamarine gets its colour from the presence of the elements chromium and iron.

Tourmaline

Boron aluminium silicate with many other atoms $Na(Mg,Fe)_3Al_6(BO_3)_3(Si_6O_{18})(OH,F)_4$

Colour: Black, but also green and pink with impurities

Hardness: 7

Cleavage: None

Crystals: Hexagonal; usually needle-shaped with well-marked striations (scratch marks); often with triangular cross-section

Streak: White

Other: Specific gravity 3.0–3.3. Found in many igneous and metamorphic rocks and in hydrothermal deposits.

The name tourmaline is from *touramalli*, a Singhalese word meaning stones of mixed colours, because it occurs as many-coloured gem pebbles in placer deposits in Sri Lanka.

The crystals are hard and have a glassy lustre.

Tourmaline, showing striations

Chain silicates

Many silica molecules form long chains. They are very strong in the direction of the chain, but they are much weaker between chains. This means that they tend to break parallel to the chains. The chain silicates mainly belong to the pyroxene or amphibole groups.

The pyroxenes are an extensive group of minerals. They are the major component of basaltic lava, the most common rock at the earth's surface (it underlies all the world's oceans). Thus pyroxenes, though not widely known, are among the most common minerals.

The most frequently seen pyroxene mineral is augite.

Amphiboles have the same chemical composition as the pyroxenes, but they form at a lower temperature. The most common mineral of this group is hornblende, found in all basalts.

Because most basalts cool quickly, only small crystals form in them, so it is usually very difficult to distinguish between the pyroxenes and amphiboles, since both look like small, dark crystals.

(Below) This diagram represents a chain silicate unit.

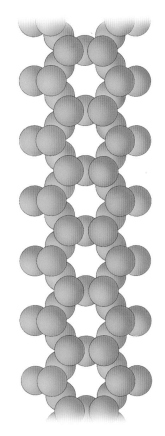

Augite

Calcium, magnesium, iron and aluminium silicate
$Ca,Na(Mg,Fe,Al)(Al,Si)_2O_6$

Colour: Green, greenish grey, black

Hardness: 6

Cleavage: Two directions at nearly right angles

Crystals: Monoclinic; mostly in small prisms

Streak: Greenish

Other: Specific gravity 3.2–3.6. A common mineral in most igneous rocks and particularly common in basic rocks.

The name augite is from the Greek word *augites*, meaning 'brightness'. This is a reference to the glassy lustre of the crystals.

Augite

Diopside

Calcium magnesium silicate $CaMgSi_2O_6$

Colour: Light green or white, vitreous

Hardness: 6

Cleavage: Good; two directions and nearly right angles

Crystals: Monoclinic; mostly in small prisms

Streak: Greenish

Other: Specific gravity 3.3–3.6. It occurs in dolomite (and thus in marble on metamorphism). Found in metamorphic rocks that have been subject to deep burial and heating rather than pressure. It is also found in areas of contact metamorphism. It is often the green-coloured mineral in marble.

The name diopside is from the Greek words *di*, meaning 'two' and *opsis*, meaning 'appearance' because the crystals normally have two sets of similar faces. This is a reference to the glassy lustre of the crystals.

Jadeite

Sodium aluminium silicate $NaAl_3Si_2O_6$

Colour: Apple green, emerald green or white

Hardness: 7

Cleavage: Distinct, two directions

Crystals: Monoclinic

Streak: White

Other: Specific gravity 3.4. A common metamorphic mineral in schists and in hydrothermal deposits, often in massive form. Semi-transparent pieces are called jade.

The name jade is from the Spanish *piedra de ijada*, meaning 'stone of the side'. This name was used because it was believed that jadeite would cure kidney diseases if placed against the side of the body. Jade is a combination of a chain of silica molecules with sodium and aluminium. The green colour is produced by atoms of iron.

Jade does not occur as crystals, but rather in a massive form, which is what makes it suitable for carving.

Diopside

Hornblende

Sodium, potassium, calcium, magnesium, iron aluminium silicate $(Ca,Na,K)_{2-3}(Mg,Fe^{2+},Fe^{3+}Al)_5(Si,Al)_8O_{22}(OH)_2$

Colour: Dark greenish-black

Hardness: 6

Cleavage: Perfect, two directions

Crystals: Monoclinic; mostly in small prisms with diamond-shaped cross-section

Streak: Colourless

Other: Specific gravity 3.0–3.4. A common mineral in most igneous rocks as shiny flakes.

The name hornblende is from the German word *horn*, meaning 'peaked' and blenden, meaning 'to deceive' (because when present it looks like a metal ore but produces no useful metal).

Jadeite

Hornblende

Sheet silicates

Many silica molecules form extensive sheets. Stacks of these sheets are connected together by metal ions; potassium and magnesium are among the most common.

Sheet silicates all break up into thin flakes. Water molecules can be absorbed between the sheets of many clay minerals.

Mica is the third most common group of minerals in the earth's crust, after quartz and the feldspars. Varieties of mica are black biotite and brown muscovite.

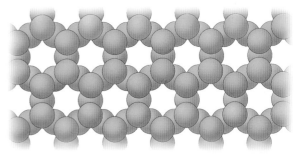

(Above) This diagram represents a sheet silicate unit.

The sheets of this mica sample are so thin that you can see through them.

Biotite

Potassium, iron, magnesium, aluminium silicate $K(Mg,Fe)_3(Al,Fe)_3Si_3O_{10}(OH,F)_2$

Colour: Black
Hardness: 3
Cleavage: Perfect, one direction
Crystals: Monoclinic; mostly as tabular crystals
Streak: Colourless
Other: Specific gravity 2.8–3.4. A common mineral in igneous (especially granite) rocks and some metamorphic rocks as small, dark, reflective flecks.

Biotite was named after a French scientist, J B Biot.

Biotite

Chlorite

A group name whose general formula is iron, magnesium, aluminium silicate $(Mg,Fe)_6(AlSi_3)O_{10}(OH)_8$

Colour: Dark green
Hardness: 2
Cleavage: Perfect, one direction
Crystals: Monoclinic; mostly as tabular crystals
Streak: Colourless
Other: Specific gravity 2.6–3.3. Found in some igneous and metamorphic rocks as small flakes.

The name chlorite is from the Greek word *chloros*, meaning 'green'.

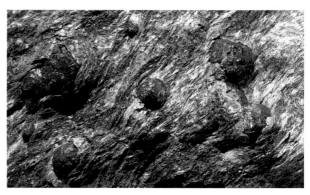

▲ Chlorite is the main green colouring mineral in this schist rock. (The red crystals are garnet.)

Muscovite

Potassium aluminium silicate $KAl_3Si_3O_{10}(OH)_2$

Colour: White, brown, colourless

Hardness: 2

Cleavage: Perfect, one direction

Crystals: Monoclinic; mostly as tabular crystals

Streak: Colourless

Other: Specific gravity 2.7. A common mineral in igneous and metamorphic rocks as shiny flakes.

The name muscovite is from Moscovy glass because it was once used instead of glass in Russia. As thin sheets it is almost transparent and is known as isinglass. It is sometimes used for furnace windows.

Muscovite

Serpentine

A group name whose general formula is magnesium silicate, sometimes with iron $(Mg,Fe)_3Si_2O_5(OH)_4$

Colour: Dark olive green

Hardness: 4

Cleavage: None in chrysotile; conchoidal fracture

Crystals: Monoclinic

Streak: White

Other: Specific gravity 2.5–2.6

The name serpentine is taken from the fact that the rocks containing serpentine (known as serpentinite) often look similar to a snake's (serpent's) skin.

Serpentine minerals are formed from the addition of hot water to magnesium silicate. It is a mineral formed under pressure and is only found in mountain systems. It is often formed from the re-melting of peridotite and has much the same chemical composition as olivine,

from which it may have been formed.

It is a noticeably soft mineral. It also has a greasy feel.

Serpentines often occur as fibrous minerals and are called 'asbestos'. Chrysotile, the fibrous form of the mineral group serpentine, accounts for about 95% of all asbestos used.

Most serpentine is green or a greyish colour. The green colour is due to the iron content. However, chrysotile is a yellowish colour.

Serpentine

Talc

Magnesium silicate $Mg_3Si_4O_{10}(OH)_2$

Colour: White, brown, or green

Hardness: 1

Cleavage: Perfect, one direction

Crystals: Monoclinic, but crystals are uncommon. Mainly occurs as thin flakes with a greasy feel

Streak: White

Other: Specific gravity 2.7. A common mineral in metamorphic rocks that have been created from dolomite (magnesium carbonate), where it occurs in schists.

Another word for talc is soapstone. The word talc comes from the Arabic word *talq*, meaning 'mica'.

Talc

Glossary

aa lava: a type of lava with a broken, bouldery surface.

abrasion: the rubbing away (erosion) of a rock by the physical scraping of particles carried by water, wind or ice.

acidic rock: a type of igneous rock that consists predominantly of light-coloured minerals and more than two-thirds silica (e.g. granite).

active volcano: a volcano that has observable signs of activity, for example, periodic plumes of steam.

adit: a horizontal tunnel drilled into rock.

aftershock: an earthquake that follows the main shock. Major earthquakes are followed by a number of aftershocks that decrease in frequency with time.

agglomerate: a rock made from the compacted particles thrown out by a volcano (e.g. tuff).

alkaline rock: a type of igneous rock containing less than half silica and normally dominated by dark-coloured minerals (e.g. gabbro).

amygdule: a vesicle in a volcanic rock filled with secondary minerals such as calcite, quartz or zeolite.

andesite: an igneous volcanic rock. Slightly more acidic than basalt.

anticline: an arching fold of rock layers in which the rocks slope down from the crest. *See also* syncline.

Appalachian Mountain (Orogenic) Belt: an old mountain range that extends for more than 3000 km along the eastern margin of North America from Alabama in the southern United States to Newfoundland, Canada, in the north. There were three Appalachian orogenies: Taconic (about 460 million years ago) in the Ordovician; Acadian (390 to 370 million years ago) in the Devonian; and Alleghenian (300 to 250 million years ago) in the Late Carboniferous to Permian. These mountain belts can be traced as the Caledonian and Hercynian orogenic belts in Europe.

Archean Eon: *see* eon.

arenaceous: a rock composed largely of sand grains.

argillaceous: a rock composed largely of clay.

arkose: a coarse sandstone formed by the disintegration of a granite.

ash, volcanic: fine powdery material thrown out of a volcano.

asthenosphere: the weak part of the upper mantle below the lithosphere, in which slow convection is thought to take place.

augite: a dark green-coloured silicate mineral containing calcium, sodium, iron, aluminium and magnesium.

axis of symmetry: a line or plane around which one part of a crystal is a mirror image of another part.

basalt: basic fine-grained igneous volcanic rock; lava often contains vesicles.

basic rock: an igneous rock (e.g. gabbro) with silica content less than two-thirds and containing a high percentage of dark-coloured minerals.

basin: a large, circular, or oval sunken region on the earth's surface created by downwards folding. A river basin, or watershed, is the area drained by a river and its tributaries.

batholith: a very large body of plutonic rock that was intruded deep into the earth's crust and is now exposed by erosion.

bauxite: a surface material that contains a high percentage of aluminium silicate. The principal ore of aluminium.

bed: a layer of sediment. It may involve many phases of deposition, each marked by a bedding plane.

bedding plane: an ancient surface on which sediment built up. Sedimentary rocks often split along bedding planes.

biotite: a black-coloured form of mica.

body wave: a seismic wave that can travel through the interior of the earth. P waves and S waves are body waves.

boss: an upwards extension of a batholith. A boss may once have been a magma chamber.

botryoidal: the shape of a mineral that resembles a bunch of grapes, e.g. haematite the crystals of which are often arranged in massive clumps, giving a surface covered with spherical bulges.

butte: a small mesa.

calcareous: composed mainly of calcium carbonate.

calcite: a mineral composed of calcium carbonate.

caldera: the collapsed cone of a volcano. It sometimes contains a crater lake.

Caledonian Mountain-Building Period, Caledonian Orogeny: a major mountain-building period in the Lower Paleozoic Era that reached its climax at the end of the Silurian Period (430 to 395 million years ago). An early phase affected only North America and made part of the Appalachian Mountain Belt.

Cambrian, Cambrian Period: the first period of geological time in the Paleozoic Era, beginning 570 million years ago and ending 500 million years ago.

carbonate minerals: minerals formed with carbonate ions (e.g. calcite).

Carboniferous, Carboniferous Period: a period of geological time between about 345 and 280 million years ago. It is often divided into the Early Carboniferous Epoch (345 to 320 million years ago) and the Late Carboniferous Epoch (320 to 280 million years ago). The Late Carboniferous is characterised by large coal-forming swamps. In North America the Carboniferous is usually divided into the Mississippian (= Lower Carboniferous) and Pennsylvanian (= Upper Carboniferous) periods.

cast, fossil: the natural filling of a mould by sediment or minerals that were left when a fossil dissolved after being enclosed by rock.

Cenozoic, Cenozoic Era: the most recent era of geological time, beginning 65 million years ago and continuing to the present.

central vent volcano: *see* stratovolcano.

chemical compound: a substance made from the chemical combination of two or more elements.

chemical rock: a rock produced by chemical precipitation (e.g. halite).

chemical weathering: the decay of a rock through the chemical action of water containing dissolved acidic gases.

cinder cone: a volcanic cone made entirely of cinders. Cinder cones have very steep sides.

class: the level of biological classification below a phylum.

clast: an individual grain of a rock.

clastic rock: a sedimentary rock that is made up of fragments of pre-existing rocks, carried by gravity, water, or wind (e.g. conglomerate, sandstone).

cleavage: the tendency of some minerals to break along one or more smooth surfaces.

coal: the carbon-rich, solid mineral derived from fossilised plant remains. Found in sedimentary rocks. Types of coal include bituminous, brown, lignite, and anthracite. A fossil fuel.

complex volcano: a volcano that has had an eruptive history and which produces two or more vents.

composite volcano: *see* stratovolcano.

concordant coast: a coast where the geological structure is parallel to the coastline. *See also* discordant coastline.

conduction (of heat): the transfer of heat between touching objects.

conglomerate: a coarse-grained sedimentary rock with grains larger than 2mm.

contact metamorphism: metamorphism that occurs owing to direct contact with a molten magma. *See also* regional metamorphism.

continental drift: the theory suggested by Alfred Wegener that earth's continents were originally one land mass which split up to form the arrangement of continents we see today.

continental shelf: the ocean floor from the coastal shore of continents to the continental slope.

continental shield: the ancient and stable core of a tectonic plate. Also called a shield.

convection: the slow overturning of a liquid or gas that is heated from below.

cordillera: a long mountain belt consisting of many mountain ranges.

core: the innermost part of the earth. The earth's core is very dense, rich in iron, partly molten, and the source of the earth's magnetic field. The inner core is solid and has a radius of about 1300 kilometres. The outer core is fluid and is about 2100 kilometres thick. S waves cannot travel through the outer core.

cracking: the breaking up of a hydrocarbon compound into simpler constituents by means of heat.

crater lake: a lake found inside a caldera.

craton: *see* shield.

Cretaceous, Cretaceous Period: the third period of the Mesozoic Era. It lasted from about 135 to 65 million years ago. It was a time of chalk formation and when many dinosaurs lived.

cross-bedding: a pattern of deposits in a sedimentary rock in which many thin layers lie at an angle to the bedding planes, showing that the sediment was deposited by a moving fluid. Wind-deposited cross-beds are often bigger than water-deposited beds.

crust: the outermost layer of the earth, typically 5 km under the oceans and 50 to 100 km thick under continents. It makes up less than 1 per cent of the earth's volume.

crustal plate: *see* tectonic plate.

crystal: a mineral that has a regular geometric shape and is bounded by smooth, flat faces.

crystal system: a group of crystals with the same arrangement of axes.

crystalline: a mineral that has solidified but has been unable to produce well-formed crystals. Quartz and halite are commonly found as crystalline masses.

crystallisation: the formation of crystals.

cubic: a crystal system in which crystals have 3 axes all at right angles to one another and of equal length.

cuesta: a ridge in the landscape formed by a resistant band of dipping rock. A cuesta has a steep scarp slope and a more gentle dip slope.

current bedding: a pattern of deposits in a sedimentary rock in which many thin layers lie at an angle to the bedding planes, showing that the sediment was deposited by a current of water.

cyclothem: a repeating sequence of rocks found in coal strata.

delta: a triangle of deposition produced where a river enters a sea or lake.

deposit, deposition: the process of laying down material that has been transported in suspension or solution by water, ice, or wind. A deposit is the material laid down by deposition (e.g. salt deposits).

destructive plate boundary: a line where plates collide and where one plate is subducted into the mantle.

Devonian, Devonian Period: the fourth period of geological time in the Palaeozoic Era, from 395 to 345 million years ago.

diorite: an igneous plutonic rock between gabbro and granite; the plutonic equivalent of andesite.

dip: the angle that a bedding plane or fault makes with the horizontal.

dip slope: the more gently sloping part of a cuesta whose surface often parallels the dip of the strata.

discontinuity: a gap in deposition, perhaps caused by the area being lifted above the sea so that erosion, rather than deposition, occurred for a time.

discordant coast: a coast where the rock structure is at an angle to the line of the coast. *See also* concordant coastline.

displacement: the distance over which one piece of rock is pushed relative to another.

dissolve: to break down a substance into a solution without causing a reaction.

distillation: the boiling off of volatile materials, leaving a residue.

dolomite: a mineral composed of calcium magnesium carbonate.

dome: a circular, uplifted region of rocks taking the shape of a dome and found in some areas of folded rocks. Rising plugs of salt will also dome up the rocks above them. They sometimes make oil traps.

dormant volcano: a volcano that shows no signs of activity but which has been active in the recent past.

drift: a tunnel drilled in rock and designed to provide a sloping route for carrying out ore or coal by means of a conveyor belt.

dyke: a wall-like sheet of igneous rock that cuts across the layers of the surrounding rocks.

dyke swarm: a collection of hundreds or thousands of parallel dykes.

earthquake: shaking of the earth's surface caused by a sudden movement of rock within the earth.

element: a fundamental chemical building block. A substance that cannot be separated into simpler substances by any chemical means. Oxygen and sulphur are examples of elements.

eon: the largest division of geological time. An eon is subdivided into eras. Precambrian time is divided into the Archean (earlier than 2.5 billion years ago) and Proterozoic eons (more recent than 2.5 billion years ago). The Phanerozoic Eon includes the Cambrian Period to the present.

epicentre: the point on the earth's surface directly above the focus (hypocentre) of an earthquake.

epoch: a subdivision of a geological period in the geological time scale (e.g. Pleistocene Epoch).

era: a subdivision of a geological eon in the geological time scale (e.g. Cenozoic Era). An era is subdivided into periods.

erode, erosion: the twin processes of breaking down a rock (called weathering) and then removing the debris (called transporting).

escarpment: the crest of a ridge made of dipping rocks.

essential mineral: the dominant mineral constituents of a rock used to classify it.

evaporite: a mineral or rock formed as the result of evaporation of salt-laden water, such as a lagoon or salt lake.

exoskeleton: another word for shell. Applies to invertebrates.

extinct volcano: a volcano that has shown no signs of activity in historic times.

extrusive rock, extrusion: an igneous volcanic rock that has solidified on the surface of the earth.

facet: the cleaved face of a mineral. Used in describing jewellery.

facies: physical, chemical, or biological variations in a sedimentary bed of the same geological age (e.g. sandy facies, limestone facies).

family: a part of the classification of living things above a genus.

fault: a deep fracture or zone of fractures in rocks along which there has been displacement of one side relative to the other. It represents a weak point in the crust and upper mantle.

fault scarp: a long, straight, steep slope in the landscape that has been produced by faulting.

feldspar: the most common silicate mineral. It consists of two forms: plagioclase and orthoclase.

ferromagnesian mineral: dark-coloured minerals, such as augite and hornblende, which contain relatively high proportions of iron and magnesium and low proportions of silica.

fissure: a substantial crack in a rock.

fjord: a glaciated valley in a mountainous area coastal area that has been partly flooded by the sea.

focal depth: the depth of an earthquake focus below the surface.

focus: the origin of an earthquake, directly below the epicentre.

fold: arched or curved rock strata.

fold axis: line following the highest arching in an anticline, or the lowest arching in a syncline.

fold belt: a part of a mountain system containing folded sedimentary rocks.

foliation: a texture of a rock (usually schist) that resembles the pages in a book.

formation: a word used to describe a collection of related rock layers or beds. A number of related beds make a member; a collection of related members makes up a formation. Formations are often given location names, e.g. Toroweap Formation, the members of which are a collection of dominantly limestone beds.

fossil: any evidence of past life, including remains, traces and imprints.

fossil fuel: any fuel that was formed in the geological past from the remains of living organisms. The main fossil fuels are coal and petroleum (oil and natural gas).

fraction: one of the components of crude oil that can be separated from others by heating and then by cooling the vapour.

fracture: a substantial break across a rock.

fracture zone: a region in which fractures are common. Fracture zones are particularly common in folded rock and near faults.

frost shattering: the process of breaking pieces of rock through the action of freezing and melting of rainwater

gabbro: alkaline igneous plutonic rock, typically showing dark-coloured crystals; plutonic equivalent of basalt.

gallery: a horizontal access tunnel in a mine.

gangue: the unwanted mineral matter found in association with a metal.

gem: a mineral, usually in crystal form, that is regarded as having particular beauty and value.

genus: (*pl.* genera) the biological classification for a group of closely related species.

geode: a hollow lump of rock (nodule) that often contains crystals.

geological column: a columnar diagram showing the divisions of geological time (eons, eras, periods, and epochs).

geological eon: *see* eon.

geological epoch: *see* epoch.

geological era: *see* era.

geological period: a subdivision of a geological era (e.g. Carboniferous Period). A period is subdivided into epochs.

geological system: a term for an accumulation of strata that occurs during a geological period (e.g. the Ordovician System is the rocks deposited during the Ordovician Period). Systems are divided into series.

geological time: the history of the earth revealed by its rocks.

geological time scale: the division of geological time into eons, era, periods, and epochs.

geosyncline: a large, slowly subsiding region marginal to a continent where huge amounts of sediment accumulate. The rocks in a geosyncline are eventually lifted to form mountain belts.

gneiss: a metamorphic rock showing large grains.

graben: a fallen block of the earth's crust forming a long trough, separated on all sides by faults. Associated with rift valleys.

grain: a particle of a rock or mineral.

granite: an acidic, igneous, plutonic rock containing free quartz, typically light in colour; plutonic equivalent of rhyolite.

grit: grains larger than sand but smaller than stones.

groundmass: *see* matrix.

group: a word used to describe a collection of related rock layers, or beds. A number of related beds make a member; a collection of related members makes up a formation; a collection of related formations makes a group.

gypsum: a mineral made of calcium sulphate.

halide minerals: a group of minerals (e.g. halite) that contain a halogen element (elements similar to chlorine) bonded with another element. Many are evaporite minerals.

halite: a mineral made of sodium chloride.

Hawaiian-type eruption: a name for a volcanic eruption that mainly consists of lava fountains.

hexagonal: a crystal system in which crystals have 3 axes all at 120 degrees to one another and of equal length.

hogback: a cuesta where the scarp and dip slopes are at about the same angle.

hornblende: a dark-green silicate mineral of the amphibole group containing sodium, potassium, calcium, magnesium, iron and aluminium.

horst: a raised block of the earth's crust separated on all sides by faults. Associated with rift valleys.

hot spot: a place where a fixed mantle magma plume reaches the surface.

hydraulic action: the erosive action of water pressure on rocks.

hydrothermal: a change brought about in a rock or mineral due to the action of superheated mineral-rich fluids, usually water.

hypocentre: the calculated location of the focus of an earthquake.

ice wedging: *see* frost shattering.

Icelandic-type eruption: a name given to a fissure type of eruption.

igneous rock: rock formed by the solidification of magma. Igneous rocks include volcanic and plutonic rocks.

impermeable: a rock that will not allow a liquid to pass through it.

imprint: a cast left by a former life form.

impurities: small amounts of elements or compounds in an otherwise homogeneous mineral.

index fossil: a fossil used as a marker for a particular part of geological time.

intrusive rock, intrusion: rocks that have formed from cooling magma below the surface. When inserted amongst other rocks, intruded rocks are called an intrusion.

invertebrate: an animal with an external skeleton.

ion: a charged particle.

island arc: a pattern of volcanic islands that follows the shape of an arc when seen from above.

isostacy: the principle that a body can float in a more dense fluid. The same as buoyancy, but used for continents.

joint: a significant crack between blocks of rock, normally used in the context of patterns of cracks.

Jurassic, Jurassic Period: the second geological period in the Mesozoic Era, lasting from about 190 to 135 million years ago.

kingdom: the broadest division in the biological classification of living things.

laccolith: a lens-shaped body of intrusive igneous rock with a dome-shaped upper surface and a flat bottom surface.

landform: a recognisable shape of part of the landscape, for example, a cuesta.

landslide: the rapid movement of a slab of soil down a steep hillslope.

lateral fault: *see* thrust fault.

laterite: a surface deposit containing a high proportion of iron.

lava: molten rock material extruded onto the surface of the earth.

lava bomb: *see* volcanic bomb.

law of superposition: the principle that younger rock is deposited on older.

limestone: a carbonate sedimentary rock composed of more than half calcium carbonate.

lithosphere: that part of the crust and upper mantle which is brittle and makes up the tectonic plates.

lode: a mining term for a rock containing many rich ore-bearing minerals. Similar to vein.

Love wave, L wave: a major type of surface earthquake wave that shakes the ground surface at right angles to the direction in which the wave is travelling. It is named after A.E.H. Love, the English mathematician who discovered it.

lustre: the way in which a mineral reflects light. Used as a test when identifying minerals.

magma: the molten material that comes from the mantle and which cools to form igneous rocks.

magma chamber: a large cavity melted in the earth's crust and filled with magma. Many magma chambers are plumes of magma that have melted their way from the mantle to the upper part of the crust. When a magma chamber is no longer supplied with molten magma, the magma solidifies to form a granite batholith.

mantle: the layer of the earth between the crust and the core. It is approximately 2900 kilometres thick and is the largest of the earth's major layers.

marginal accretion: the growth of mountain belts on the edges of a shield.

mass extinction: a time when the majority of species on the planet were killed off.

matrix: the rock or sediment in which a fossil is embedded; the fine-grained rock in which larger particles are embedded, for example, in a conglomerate.

mechanical weathering: the disintegration of a rock by frost shattering/ice wedging.

mesa: a large detached piece of a tableland.

Mesozoic, Mesozoic Era: the geological era between the Palaeozoic and the Cenozoic eras. It lasted from about 225 to 65 million years ago.

metamorphic aureole: the region of contact metamorphic rock that surrounds a batholith.

metamorphic rock: any rock (e.g. schist, gneiss) that was formed from a pre-existing rock by heat and pressure.

meteorite: a substantial chunk of rock in space.

micas: a group of soft, sheet-like silicate minerals (e.g. biotite, muscovite).

mid-ocean ridge: a long mountain chain on the ocean floor where basalt periodically erupts, forming new oceanic crust.

mineral: a naturally occurring inorganic substance of definite chemical composition (e.g. calcite, calcium carbonate).
More generally, any resource extracted from the ground by mining (includes metal ores, coal, oil, gas, rocks, etc.).

mineral environment: the place where a mineral or a group of associated minerals form. Mineral environments include igneous, sedimentary, and metamorphic rocks.

mineralisation: the formation of minerals within a rock.

Modified Mercalli Scale: a scale for measuring the impact of an earthquake. It is composed of 12 increasing levels of intensity, which range from imperceptible, designated by Roman numeral I, to catastrophic destruction, designated by XII.

Mohorovicic discontinuity: the boundary surface that separates the earth's crust from the underlying mantle. Named after Andrija Mohorovicic, a Croatian seismologist.

Mohs' Scale of Hardness: a relative scale developed to put minerals into an order. The hardest is 10 (diamond), and the softest is 1 (talc).

monoclinic: a crystal system in which crystals have 2 axes all at right angles to one another, and each axis is of unequal length.

mould: an impression in a rock of the outside of an organism.

mountain belt: a region where there are many ranges of mountains. The term is often applied to a wide belt of mountains produced during mountain building.

mountain building: the creation of mountains as a result of the collision of tectonic plates. Long belts or chains of mountains can form along the edge of a continent during this process. Mountain building is also called orogeny.

mountain building period: a period during which a geosyncline is compressed into fold mountains by the collision of two tectonic plates. Also known as orogenesis.

mudstone: a fine-grained, massive rock formed by the compaction of mud.

nappe: a piece of a fold that has become detached from its roots during intensive mountain building.

native metal: a metal that occurs uncombined with any other element.

natural gas: *see* petroleum.

normal fault: a fault in which one block has slipped down the face of another. It is the most common kind of fault and results from tension.

nueé ardente: another word for pyroclastic flow.

ocean trench: a deep, steep-sided trough in the ocean floor caused by the subduction of oceanic crust beneath either other oceanic crust or continental crust.

olivine: the name of a group of magnesium iron silicate minerals that have an olive colour.

order: a level of biological classification between class and family.

Ordovician, Ordovician Period: the second period of geological time within the Palaeozoic Era. It lasted from about 500 to 430 million years ago.

ore: a rock containing enough useful metal or fuel to be worth mining.

ore mineral: a mineral that occurs in sufficient quantity to be mined for its metal. The compound must also be easy to process.

organic rocks: rocks formed by living things, for example, coal.

orthoclase: the form of feldspar that is often pink in colour and which contains potassium as important ions.

orogenic belt: a mountain belt.

orogeny: a period of mountain building. Orogenesis is the process of mountain building and the creation of orogenic belts.

orthorhombic: a crystal system in which crystals have 3 axes all at right angles to one another but of unequal length.

outcrop: the exposure of a rock at the surface of the earth.

overburden: the unwanted layer(s) of rock above an ore or coal body.

oxide minerals: a group of minerals in which oxygen is a major constituent. A compound in which oxygen is bonded to another element or group.

Pacific Ring of Fire: the ring of volcanoes and volcanic activity that circles the Pacific Ocean. Created by the collision of the Pacific Plate with its neighbouring plates.

pahoehoe lava: the name for a form of lava that has a smooth surface.

Palaeozoic, Palaeozoic Era: a major interval of geological time. The Palaeozoic is the oldest era in which fossil life is commonly found. It lasted from about 570 to 225 million years ago.

palaeomagnetism: the natural magnetic traces that reveal the intensity and direction of the earth's magnetic field in the geological past.

pegmatite: an igneous rock (e.g. a dyke) of extremely coarse crystals.

Pelean-type eruption: a violent explosion dominated by pyroclastic flows.

period: *see* geological period.

permeable rock: a rock that will allow a fluid to pass through it.

Permian, Permian Period: the last period of the Palaeozoic Era, lasting from about 280 to 225 million years ago.

petrified: when the tissues of a dead plant or animal have been replaced by minerals, such as silica, they are said to be petrified (e.g. petrified wood).

petrified forest: a large number of fossil trees. Most petrified trees are replaced by silica.

petroleum: the carbon-rich, and mostly liquid, mixture produced by the burial and partial alteration of animal and plant remains. Petroleum is found in many sedimentary rocks. The liquid part of petroleum is called oil, the gaseous part is known as natural gas. Petroleum is an important fossil fuel.

petroleum field: a region from which petroleum can be recovered.

Phanerozoic Eon: the most recent eon, beginning at the Cambrian Period, some 570 million years ago, and extending up to the present.

phenocryst: an especially large crystal (in a porphyritic rock), embedded in smaller mineral grains.

phylum: (*pl.* phyla) biological classification for one of the major divisions of animal life and second in complexity to kingdom. The plant kingdom is not divided into phyla but into divisions.

placer deposit: a sediment containing heavy metal grains (e.g. gold) that have weathered out of the bedrock and are concentrated on a stream bed or along a coast.

plagioclase: the form of feldspar that is often white or grey and which contains sodium and calcium as important ions.

planetismals: small embryo planets.

plate: *see* tectonic plate.

plateau: an extensive area of raised flat land. The cliff-like edges of a plateau may, when eroded, leave isolated features such as mesas and buttes. *See also* tableland.

plate tectonics: the theory that the earth's crust and upper mantle (the lithosphere) are broken into a number of more or less rigid, but constantly moving, slabs or plates.

Plinian-type eruption: an explosive eruption that sends a column of ash high into the air.

plug: *see* volcanic plug

plunging fold: a fold whose axis dips, or plunges, into the ground.

plutonic rock: an igneous rock that has solidified at great depth and contains large crystals due to the slowness of cooling (e.g. granite, gabbro).

porphyry, porphyritic rock: an igneous rock in which larger crystals (phenocrysts) are enclosed in a fine-grained matrix.

Precambrian, Precambrian time: the whole of earth history before the Cambrian Period. Also called Precambrian Era and Precambrian Eon.

precipitate: a substance that has settled out of a liquid as a result of a chemical reaction between two chemicals in the liquid.

Primary Era: an older name for the Palaeozoic Era.

prismatic: a word used to describe a mineral that has formed with one axis very much longer than the others.

Proterozoic Eon: *see* eon.

P wave, primary wave, primary seismic wave: P waves are the fastest body waves. The waves carry energy in the same line as the direction of the wave. P waves can travel through all layers of the earth and are generally felt as a thump. *See also* S wave.

pyrite: iron sulphide. It is common in sedimentary rocks that were poor in oxygen, and sometimes forms fossil casts.

pyroclastic flow: solid material ejected from a volcano, combined with searingly hot gases, which together behave as a high-density fluid. Pyroclastic flows can do immense damage, as was the case with Mount Saint Helens.

pyroclastic material: any solid material ejected from a volcano.

Quaternary, Quaternary Period: the second period in the Cenozoic Era, beginning about 1.6 million years ago and continuing to the present day.

radiation: the transfer of energy between objects that are not in contact.

radioactive dating: the dating of a material by the use of its radioactive elements. The rate of decay of any element changes in a predictable way, allowing a precise date to be given of when the material was formed.

rank: a name used to describe the grade of coal in terms of its possible heat output. The higher the rank, the more the heat output.

Rayleigh wave: a type of surface wave having an elliptical motion similar to the waves caused when a stone is dropped into a pond. It is the slowest, but often the largest and most destructive, of the wave types caused by an earthquake. It is usually felt as a rolling or rocking motion and, in the case of major earthquakes, can be seen as they approach. Named after Lord Rayleigh, the English physicist who predicted its existence.

regional metamorphism: metamorphism resulting from both heat and pressure. It is usually connected with mountain building and occurs over a large area. *See also* contact metamorphism.

reniform: a kidney-shaped mineral habit (e.g. hematite).

reservoir rock: a permeable rock in which petroleum accumulates.

reversed fault: a fault where one slab of the earth's crust rides up over another. Reversed faults are only common during plate collision.

rhyolite: acid, igneous, volcanic rock, typically light in colour; volcanic equivalent of granite.

ria: the name for a partly flooded coastal river valley in an area where the landscape is hilly.

Richter Scale: the system used to measure the strength of an earthquake. Developed by Charles Richter, an American, in 1935.

rift, rift valley: long troughs on continents and mid-ocean ridges that are bounded by normal faults.

rifting: the process of crustal stretching that causes blocks of crust to subside, creating rift valleys.

rock: a naturally occurring solid material containing one or more minerals.

rock cycle: the continuous sequence of events that cause mountains to be formed, then eroded, before being formed again.

rupture: the place over which an earthquake causes rocks to move against one another.

salt dome: a balloon-shaped mass of salt produced by salt being forced upwards under pressure.

sandstone: a sedimentary rock composed of cemented sand-sized grains 0.06–2 mm in diameter.

scarp slope: the steep slope of a cuesta.

schist: a metamorphic rock characterised by a shiny surface of mica crystals all orientated in the same direction.

scoria: the rough, often foam-like rock that forms on the surface of some lavas.

seamount: a volcano that rises from the sea bed.

Secondary Era: an older term for a geological era. Now replaced by Mesozoic Era.

sediment: any solid material that has settled out of suspension in a liquid.

sedimentary rock: a layered clastic rock formed through the deposition of pieces of mineral, rock, animal or vegetable matter.

segregation: the separation of minerals.

seismic gap: a part of an active fault where there have been no earthquakes in recent times.

seismic wave: a wave generated by an earthquake.

series: the rock layers that correspond to an epoch of time.

shadow zone: the region of the earth that experiences no shocks after an earthquake.

shaft: a vertical tunnel that provides access or ventilation to a mine.

shale: a fine-grained sedimentary rock made of clay minerals with particle sizes smaller than 2 microns.

shield: the ancient and stable core of a tectonic plate. Also called a continental shield.

shield volcano: a volcano with a broad, low-angled cone made entirely of lava.

silica, silicate: silica is silicon dioxide. It is a very common mineral, occurring as quartz, chalcedony, etc. A silicate is any mineral that contains silica.

sill: a tabular, sheet-like body of intrusive igneous rock that has been injected between layers of sedimentary or metamorphic rock.

Silurian, Silurian Period: the name of the third geological period of the Palaeozoic Era. It began about 430 and ended about 395 million years ago.

skarn: a mineral deposit formed by the chemical reaction of hot acidic fluids and carbonate rocks.

slag: waste rock material that becomes separated from the metal during smelting.

slate: a low-grade metamorphic rock produced by pressure, in which the clay minerals have arranged themselves parallel to one another.

slaty cleavage: a characteristic pattern found in slates in which the parallel arrangement of clay minerals causes the rock to fracture (cleave) in sheets.

species: a population of animals or plants capable of interbreeding.

spreading boundary: a line where two plates are being pulled away from each other. New crust is formed as molten rock is forced upwards into the gap.

stock: a vertical protrusion of a batholith that pushes up closer to the surface.

stratigraphy: the study of the earth's rocks in the context of their history and conditions of formation.

stratovolcano: a tall volcanic mountain made of alternating layers, or strata, of ash and lava.

stratum: (*pl.* strata) a layer of sedimentary rock.

streak: the colour of the powder of a mineral produced by rubbing the mineral against a piece of unglazed, white porcelain. Used as a test when identifying minerals.

striation: minute parallel grooves on crystal faces.

strike, direction of: the direction of a bedding plane or fault at right angles to the dip.

Strombolian-type eruption: a kind of volcanic eruption that is explosive enough

to send out some volcanic bombs.

subduction: the process of one tectonic plate descending beneath another.

subduction zone: the part of the earth's surface along which one tectonic plate descends into the mantle. It is often shaped in the form of an number of arcs.

sulphides: a group of important ore minerals (e.g. pyrite, galena, and sphalerite) in which sulphur combines with one or more metals.

surface wave: any one of a number of waves such as Love waves or Rayleigh waves that shake the ground surface just after an earthquake. *See also* Love waves and Rayleigh waves.

suture: the junction of 2 or more parts of a skeleton; in cephalopods the junction of a septum with the inner surface of the shell wall. It is very distinctive in ammonoids and used to identify them.

S wave, shear or secondary seismic wave: this kind of wave carries energy through the earth like a rope being shaken. S waves cannot travel through the outer core of the earth because they cannot pass through fluids. *See also* P wave.

syncline: a downfold of rock layers in which the rocks slope up from the bottom of the fold. *See also* anticline.

system: see geological system.

tableland: another word for a plateau. *See* plateau.

tectonic plate: one of the great slabs, or plates, of the lithosphere (the earth's crust and part of the earth's upper mantle) that covers the whole of the earth's surface. The earth's plates are separated by zones of volcanic and earthquake activity.

Tertiary, Tertiary Period: the first period of the Cenozoic Era. It began 665 and ended about 1.6 million years ago.

thrust fault: see reversed fault.

transcurrent fault: see lateral fault.

transform fault: see lateral fault.

translucent: a description of a mineral that allows light to penetrate but not pass through.

transparent: a description of a mineral that allows light to pass right through.

trellis drainage pattern: a river drainage system where the trunk river and its tributaries tend to meet at right angles.

trench: see ocean trench.

Triassic, Triassic Period: the first period of the Mesozoic era. It lasted from about 225 to 190 million years ago.

triclinic: a crystal system in which crystals have 3 axes, none at right angles or of equal length to one another.

tsunami: a very large wave produced by an underwater earthquake.

tuff: a rock made from volcanic ash.

unconformity: any interruption in the depositional sequence of sedimentary rocks.

valve: in bivalves and brachiopods, one of the separate parts of the shell.

vein: a sheet-like body of mineral matter (e.g. quartz) that cuts across a rock. Veins are often important sources of valuable minerals. Miners call such important veins lodes.

vent: the vertical pipe that allows the passage of magma through the centre of a volcano.

vertebrate: an animal with an internal skeleton.

vesicle: a small cavity in a volcanic rock originally created by an air bubble trapped in the molten lava.

viscous, viscosity: sticky, stickiness.

volatile: substances that tend to evaporate or boil off of a liquid.

volcanic: anything from, or of, a volcano. Volcanic rocks are igneous rocks that cool as they are released at the earth's surface – including those formed underwater; typically have small crystals due to the rapid cooling, e.g. basalt, andesite and rhyolite.

volcanic bomb: a large piece of magma thrown out of a crater during an eruption, which solidifies as it travels through cool air.

volcanic eruption: an ejection of ash or lava from a volcano.

volcanic glass: lava that has solidified very quickly and has not had time to develop any crystals. Obsidian is a volcanic glass.

volcanic plug: the solidified core of an extinct volcano.

Vulcanian-type eruption: an explosive form of eruption without a tall ash column or pyroclastic flow.

water gap: a gap cut by a superimposed river, which is still occupied by the river.

weather, weathered, weathering: the process of weathering is the mechanical action of ice and the chemical action of rainwater on rock, breaking it down into small pieces that can then be carried away. *See also* chemical weathering and mechanical weathering.

wind gap: a gap cut by a superimposed river, which is no longer occupied by the river.

Set Index

USING THE SET INDEX

This index covers all eight volumes in the *Earth Science* set:

Volume
number   Title

  1:   **Minerals**
  2:   **Rocks**
  3:   **Fossils**
  4:   **Earthquakes and volcanoes**
  5:   **Plate tectonics**
  6:   **Landforms**
  7:   **Geological time**
  8:   **The earth's resources**

An example entry:
    Index entries are
    listed alphabetically.

plagioclase feldspar **1:** *51*; **2:** 10 *see also*
    feldspars

Volume numbers are in bold and are followed by page references. Articles on a subject are shown by italic page numbers.
  In the example above, 'plagioclase feldspar' appears in Volume 1: Minerals on page 51 as a full article and in Volume 2: Rocks on page 10. Many terms also are covered in the GLOSSARY on pages 60–65.
  The *see also* refers to another entry where there will be additional relevant information.